JAPANESE HOT POTS

JAPANESE HOT POTS
COMFORTING ONE-POT MEALS

Tadashi Ono & Harris Salat

FOOD PHOTOGRAPHY BY LUCY SCHAEFFER | LOCATION PHOTOGRAPHY BY JUN TAKAGI

TEN SPEED PRESS
Berkeley

Published in the United States by Ten Speed Press,
an imprint of the Crown Publishing Group,
a division of Random House, Inc., New York.
www.crownpublishing.com
www.tenspeed.com

Ten Speed Press and the Ten Speed Press colophon are
registered trademarks of Random House, Inc.

Library of Congress Cataloging-in-Publication Data
Ono, Tadashi, 1962–
    Japanese hot pots : comforting one-pot meals / Tadashi Ono and
Harris Salat.
        p. cm.
    Includes index.
    Summary: "A collection of 50 recipes for authentic Japanese hot pots,
including a primer on hot pot culture, ingredients, condiments, and
tools"—Provided by publisher.
    1. One-dish meals—Japan. 2. Cookery, Japanese.
I. Salat, Harris. II. Title.
    TX840.O53O56 2009
    641.8'20952—dc22

                        2009008445

ISBN 978-1-58008-981-4
Printed in China

Cover and text design by Toni Tajima
Food styling by Martha Bernabe
Photography assistance by Shane Walsh

10 9 8 7 6 5 4 3
First Edition

Contents

CHICKEN AND DUCK 93

BEEF, PORK, LAMB, AND VENISON 113

Acknowledgments

I'D LIKE TO THANK my wonderful family—my wife, Manami, and daughters, Sueh and Kiku—for all the fun we've had sharing hot pots. They're my inspiration and the reason I cook these dishes. I'd also like to thank Sean MacPherson, Eric Goode, Mikio Shinagawa, Richard Born, and Ira Driker, the owners of Matsuri restaurant, for their support; Maurice Rodrigues of the Maritime Hotel; and Ryuji Irie, Taka Terashita, and the rest of the crew in the Matsuri kitchen.

—*Tadashi*

I'D LIKE TO THANK my lovely wife, the artist Momoyo Torimitsu, for her wisdom, encouragement, and stellar palate; my mother and grandmother for kindling my passion for cooking; my father and Uncle Adam for bequeathing a zest for storytelling and curiosity about the world; my old buddies Clark Morgan and David Seeley for mentoring my wordsmithing; and my friends and heroes Stephen and Corky Pollan for inspiring me to write about food.

—*Harris*

BOTH OF US would like to thank the amazing people across the globe who have generously helped us with this book. In no particular order, we'd like to thank our editor, Brie Mazurek, and the terrific team at Ten Speed Press; our fantastic volunteer recipe testers around the world; the good folks at Le Crueset, Lodge, and Staub for supplying us with their outstanding cookware; our literary agent, Jeremy Katz; Jim Oseland, Dana Bowen, Todd Coleman, Hunter Lewis, and the gang at *Saveur* magazine for their assistance and for lending us their props; our friends in the Japanese government for their support and encouragement; Chef Hisao Nakahigashi, his wife, Kimiko, and his son, Atsushi, for their gracious assistance in Kyoto; Mr. and Mrs. Takao Kawasaki of Fukuoka; Chef Chikara Sono of Kyo Ya in New York; Lloyd Nakano of the Hotel Seiyo Ginza in Tokyo; Chef Motohide Midorikawa; Mrs. Sachio Imai of Kyoto; Atsuko Uchida for her research and assistance; our location photographer, Jun Takagi; our food photographer, Lucy Schaeffer, and food stylist, Martha Bernabe; Yuki Sakamoto for all her help and research; journalist Keiko Tsuyama for her keen input; Michele Bonds for testing, tasting, and offering invaluable feedback; Jamie Graves and Kate Rankin for their research; author Andrea Nguyen for her sage advice; journalist Asao Teshirogi for her assistance; Kay Blumenthal for her spot-on editorial insights; Eric Shih and Stephana Patton for reading and reviewing; and the restaurants Miyako and Yoshi Ume in Tokyo, Kindaite in Ishikari, Hinote in Otaru, and Yoshioka in Fukuoka.

Introduction

I GREW UP IN the downtown section of Tokyo, home to Edokko, the Edo people—my people—a historic city subculture known for its good humor, easygoing cool, and soul. My family lived in a small house wedged beside the other modest houses in our working class neighborhood ("houses so small you never have to shout," Edokko like to say). It wasn't a fancy area, but it was always full of life. Edokko are social people, and our lives revolved around family, friends—and great food and drink.

Every morning my mother headed to local markets to spend what she could to buy the freshest vegetables, fish, shellfish, pork, chicken, and meat. When my father returned from his job or a gig (he was also a musician), we'd bring out our gorgeous tableware—our most prized possession—and pack our little dining room with family, my father's bandmates, and a neighbor or two to share delicious, leisurely meals. Especially hot pot meals.

Hot pots became popular in Tokyo some four centuries ago, back when it was the newly minted capital of Japan, a city then called Edo. These cozy hot pot dishes were a fundamental food in my home, the beloved cooking of my childhood: tuna belly, when my mom could find it at the market; hearty yellowtail and daikon on frigid winter days; delicate pork shabu-shabu all year round; economical hand-pulled noodles at least once a month; and expensive sukiyaki (beef was pricey) every once in a while, to celebrate a special day.

I started cooking when I was sixteen and moved to America twenty-five years ago. Today I'm a professional chef running an acclaimed restaurant in New York City. But when I take off my chef's coat and cook dinner in my family kitchen, hot pots are the dishes I always come back to. Nothing beats these humble, heartwarming meals I share with my wife and kids. It's real food that grounds me, real food that never lets me forget my roots.

—*Tadashi*

AN INVITATION TO Sunday dinner at my friend, sensei, and coauthor Tadashi's house inspired this book. My wife and I gathered around the dining table with Tadashi, his wife, and his two daughters and their sock monkeys. Platters brimmed with shrimp, glossy sea scallops, littleneck clams, and sliced red snapper waiting to be cooked. Neat mounds of napa cabbage, earthy mushrooms, green onions, bright carrots, and gleaming blocks of tofu beckoned on more trays. In the center of the table sat a portable burner, its flames warming a large clay pot bubbling with a caramel-colored broth. A heavenly soy sauce aroma filled the room.

"OK, everybody," Tadashi announced. "Let's. Do. Hot pot!"

Hot pots are the quintessential Japanese comfort food, easy one-pot meals of wholesome ingredients poached in a mouthwatering broth. They can be cooked all at once or experienced as a fun feast, like that night at Tadashi's, where each of us leisurely simmered the foods ourselves. Either way, they're a communal dish to savor with family and friends.

I first tasted hot pots in Japan, where I've been traveling for the past decade, writing about food, and studying how to cook it. I fell in love with these down-home dishes. Wherever I went, an invitation to share this cooking was a hand in welcome—breaking bread, Japanese-style. Watching his American-born daughters, fifth and sixth graders, eagerly plucking tasty vegetables and seafood from the hot pot, and just as eagerly sharing laughs at the table, Tadashi and I thought, why don't we all eat this way?

For too many of us, Japanese food means one thing—sushi. But in Japan, it's considered a restaurant treat, something sliced by a specially trained chef. Hot pots are a different story. Down-to-earth and economical, they're fundamental Japanese home cooking, simple dishes anyone can make.

Hot pots are a well-balanced and naturally nutritious bounty of roots, greens, mushrooms, onion, tofu, noodles, and chicken, seafood, or meat, all infused with lip-smacking Japanese flavors (tastes we already love in sushi). They're perfect for a crisp autumn day, and warming on icy winter nights. They're fast and easy to prepare; fun and social to share. Every corner of Japan boasts its own traditional version, so you'll find hot pots to satisfy any craving, pleasing everyone from vegetarians to meat-and-potatoes fans.

In the pages that follow, we'll explain everything you need to know to prepare these delicious one-pot meals, from basic ingredients and techniques to the simple cookware, which you already own. Then we'll introduce our favorite authentic recipes from across Japan, all designed to be easily cooked here in America. The hot pots in this book are so straightforward and forgiving, you can't mess them up. We promise. Once you start cooking them, we know you'll want to gather friends and family and weave them into the fabric of your life. Just like we do in ours.

—*Harris*

The Basics

HOT POTS, what the Japanese call *nabe* (nah-beh), are a fundamental style of Japanese home cooking, which means, by definition, they're simple, fast, and easy to prepare. Many of us, though, have almost no point of reference for Japanese food beyond the local sushi bar, so cooking this cuisine can sometimes seem exotic and intimidating. But here's a secret: with a little know-how, Japanese food is a cinch to make, especially these comforting dishes. In the pages that follow, we'll walk you though everything you need to know, from understanding essential ingredients and seasonings to choosing the right cookware to learning basic techniques. So very soon, whipping up a gorgeous hot pot will become as second nature as roasting a chicken.

WHAT IS A JAPANESE HOT POT?

Japanese hot pots are a delicious medley of foods poached in broth inside a single cooking vessel, a tempting combination of vegetables, tofu, noodles, seafood, poultry, or meat. They're usually enjoyed in the colder months, but many of these dishes are also eaten year round. They evolved in Japan as wholesome, economical, and complete one-pot meals, especially with rice or noodles added at the finish as is customary. Compared to Western foods, they're heartier than soup but not as dense as stew.

Think of hot pots as a mingling of tasty layers: broth, foundation ingredients (basic foods found in every dish), main ingredients, natural flavorings like soy sauce and miso, and accents and garnishes like wasabi. Each of these enhances the others and together they create the dish. And because the ingredients and flavorings cook in broth, they impart their essence to the liquid as well as to the other foods in the pot. So everything is nuancing everything else all the time—which is why these dishes produce such delightfully vibrant tastes even though they're so easy to make.

Let's take a peek at each of the layers to understand them better.

Broth (and Dashi)

Japanese hot pots come in three basic styles, based on the broth—water and kombu, flavored stock, or a thick broth. In the first, water simmers with kombu, a remarkable kelp (see "The Power of Kombu," page 6). Foods poached in this liquid are then dipped into a sauce to add taste. In the second, stock is combined with flavorings like soy sauce or miso (a fermented paste) to create a complex broth that infuses the foods simmering in it. No need to dip. Finally, there's a thick broth closer to a sauce than a stock, substantial enough to stand up to boldly flavored foods like beef, venison, or oysters.

Japanese-style chicken stock (page 32), mushroom stock, or even sake can form the basis of a hot pot broth, but dashi is the most common. For good reason. The Japanese word for "stock," *dashi* is both a generic term and one synonymous with the classic stock made from kombu and dried, shaved bonito (a variety of tuna). This is the dashi we refer to throughout the book.

Kombu and bonito are both naturally preserved ingredients, and both remarkable. Giant kelp that can grow several yards long, kombu is dried into ribbons the thickness of cardboard. Bonito undergoes a more extensive transformation, the fish first filleted and boiled, then smoked, covered in mold, and sun-dried to the hardness of oak, a technique dating from the 1600s. All this culinary alchemy concentrates the ample umami naturally found in both ingredients (see "The Umm in Umami," opposite page). And when they combine in dashi—incredibly—their flavor compounds synergize and pack an even greater palate-pleasing wallop.

Making dashi is straightforward: You soak and heat the kombu in water to extract its essence, remove it, then steep the bonito flakes in the liquid, like tea (see Dashi, page 30). Compared to a traditional Western stock, where bones, roots, and herbs are slow-simmered to tease out their essence, dashi is faster to prepare. And with just two ingredients, it's also lighter, so its deep savory kick magnifies other foods rather than masks them, making dashi an incredibly versatile ingredient.

The Power of Kombu

Butter may be cook's little helper in Western cuisine, but the Japanese have kombu, a truly amazing ingredient. Throughout the book, we boost the taste of hot pots—even one with a beef broth—simply by dropping in a couple of pieces of this naturally preserved kelp. Kombu does three things: it delivers a mega-hit of umami, imbues a beautiful and delicate fragrance, and gives liquid tangible body. This works even with plain water. Add kombu to water, wait a few hours, then taste, smell, and stir to notice the body, and you'll see. (Heating hastens all this.) Besides flavoring a dish, cooked kombu itself is pretty tasty. Cut it into small pieces to eat, if you'd like, or just leave it in the pot.

Kombu comes in a number of grades, varieties, and sizes, some of it very pricey. It's typically sold in the United States in ribbons about 3 inches wide (sometimes they're curled up a bit, but unfurl in liquid). The recipes in this book usually call for two 6-inch-long pieces, which together weigh $1/2$ to $3/4$ ounce, with surface area of 30 to 40 square inches. If you find kombu ribbons of different widths, just approximate the weight or area. Before using, lightly wipe the kombu with a damp cloth or paper towel if you notice any dust. But don't clean too rigorously, as the talc-like substance on its surface is an umami compound you want to keep.

The Umm in Umami

The word might seem mysterious, but you're already familiar with umami. You taste it whenever you savor a chunk of fine Parmesan, a sizzling porterhouse, or a perfectly ripe heirloom tomato—it's that mouthwatering savoriness that beckons you to bite more. Produced by natural amino acid and nucleotide flavor compounds, this lip-smacking taste is in bountiful supply in traditional Japanese ingredients like miso, soy sauce, and dashi's kombu and dried bonito. It's not by accident. For much of Japan's history, eating meat was taboo, so instead of using the animal fats and butter that enhance Western cooking, Japanese figured out inventive ways to create a meat-like savoriness in foods, but without the meat. Umami is what gives Japanese food its delicious, irresistible appeal, a flavor sensation as recognizable—and satisfying—as the umm-umm-goodness of a homemade chicken stock.

Foundation Ingredients

Every Japanese hot pot is cooked with a group of whole-some foods that bestow flavor, nutrition, and heft to the dish. These are the foundation ingredients, a humble, economical, and healthy assortment of roots, greens, onion, mushrooms, and tofu. Combine them with broth, natural flavor, and the main ingredients and you've got a deeply satisfying meal-in-a-pot. You may not be familiar with every food we describe here, but they're all age-old Japanese staples that contribute their own singular flavors and textures. (Texture is about how food feels inside your mouth, a sensation as pleasing as taste to the Japanese palate.) Also, the vegetables here are in peak season in Japan during the colder months, making them the traditional foods for this cooking. All hot pot ingredients are readily available at Japanese and Asian markets (see Resources, page 139).

Napa cabbage: A type of Chinese cabbage (and some-times called that), it's the traditional workhorse of hot pot cooking, appearing in most recipes in the book. (In most cases we specify a particular way to slice these leaves. See "How to Slice Napa Cabbage," page 52.) This nutritious Japanese staple has a delicate taste, transforming as it cooks from crispy and green to tender and sweet. While it simmers, too, its porous leaves work like a sponge to absorb broth and pull in lots of flavor. Look for crisp, fresh leaves that are yellow-green at the tips, turning white at the stem. Note that for a few hot pots, instead of napa, we use ordinary round green cabbage, also long cultivated in Japan. Green cabbage has a stronger, more pronounced flavor than napa cabbage, and isn't as tender, but it works better for certain dishes. Use the green leaves only; discard the hard white core.

Daikon: A radish that looks like a giant white carrot, daikon can grow over a foot long and as thick as a baseball bat. Look for a firm root; when squeezed, it should feel like a taut balloon. In hot pots, daikon is eaten either cooked or grated raw. When poached, it develops a delicate sweetness and readily absorbs the flavors from a dish. Grated raw it adds a refreshing counterpoint, especially when matched with rich foods like oily fish. (Raw daikon also contains natural digestive enzymes that help

Clockwise from top left: DAIKON, BURDOCK ROOT, *NEGI*, KABOCHA, TARO AND LOTUS ROOT SLICES

Clockwise from top left: *SHIMEJI*, ENOKI, SHIITAKE, AND OYSTER MUSHROOMS

assimilate said rich foods when eaten together.) When you peel a daikon, make sure to remove all of its thick, white skin to fully expose the glossy flesh. The middle of the root holds the sweetest flavor and is the best part for cooking. The tip, on the other hand, is spicy and fibrous; use it for grating. Daikon is usually precooked to soften it before it is added to a hot pot.

Negi: This remarkable onion has a sharp, acidic taste when raw that turns sweet and tender when simmered. We take advantage of both qualities in the recipes, pairing the bite of lightly poached *negi* with rich ingredients like pork belly to cut their fattiness, or cooking it all the way to add delectable sweetness to a broth. *Negi* also mellows the fishiness of seafood, adding a *sappari* (cleansing) quality to the palate, much like wasabi does for sushi. There are a number of varieties of *negi*, but we use Tokyo *negi* (also called *naga negi*), which is readily available here. Having long white cylinders that sprout green leaves, these onions grow up to $3/4$ inch thick and 2 feet long. Unless we indicate otherwise, use the entire *negi*, including the green parts, but trim off any dry leaves. This onion is sometimes called "Japanese leek" (although not a leek) or "welsh onion" (no connection to Wales), but we're sticking to *negi*, like in Japan. Finally, if you can't find them, substitute two large scallions per *negi* in the recipes.

Japanese mushrooms: Autumn in Japan heralds the arrival of crisp hot pot weather—and the start of the country's celebrated wild mushroom picking season. Japanese mushrooms lavish incomparable earthy, woody flavors and fragrance to hot pots, and add a seductive visual touch to these dishes. We use a quartet of cultivated varieties that are readily available at Japanese and Asian markets.

If you have trouble finding any of these mushrooms, substitute white button, brown crimini, or another cultivated variety of your choosing (but not portobellos,

whose flavor can overwhelm a broth). Wild edible mushrooms like trumpets and chanterelles are fantastic, too. Almost any mushroom will add fragrance and flavor to a hot pot, so feel free to give different varieties a try. To clean mushrooms, wipe off any dust and dirt with a damp paper towel or cloth. You can store them in the refrigerator for two to three days; just wrap in a paper towel and place inside a sealed container before sticking them in the fridge.

- *Shiitake* are the best known Japanese mushrooms, with the common variety of this bold fungi found in gourmet markets across the country. There's also another type of shiitake often sold at Japanese markets called *donko*, with thicker caps that curl under. If you can find *donko*, use them because they have more potent flavor. (But regular shiitake are terrific, too.) Cut off the tough stems and discard before cooking, and halve any large caps to make them bite-size. Shiitake are also sold dried, which we reconstitute in water to make a stock for some recipes. Soak these whole, stems and all.

- *Shimeji* are tender, straw-colored mushrooms that grow in clusters and have small caps that are $1/4$ to $1/2$ inch across. These mushrooms add more flavor than fragrance, infusing dishes with an appealing earthiness. They're typically sold in 100-gram packages (about $3^1/2$ ounces).

- *Enoki* are delicate white mushrooms that grow in a dense clump, with tiny white caps sitting atop long, thin stalks. They add a subtle but distinctive flavor and fragrance to hot pots. They're typically sold in 200-gram packages (about 7 ounces).

- *Oyster* is our mushroom substitute for *maitake*, a delicious fungi but difficult to find here, while oyster mushrooms are native to America. (If you come across *maitake*, you can use them instead of oyster mushrooms in the recipes.) White oyster mushrooms grow in large clusters and have irregular-shaped caps. While not as distinctively fungusy as *maitake*, they add their own appealing flavor and fragrance. Cut their large caps into more manageable pieces.

Japanese greens: Greens add nutrition, flavor, and lovely color to hot pots. We use a trio of leaves in our dishes. The first, spinach, is as popular in Japan as it is here. The other two, mizuna and *shungiku*, are less familiar to American cooks. If you can't find one or the other, you can substitute watercress (which will add its own flavor to a hot pot) or spinach for either. No matter what the leaves, make sure to wash them well to remove any sand and dirt, and always add them as the last step so they quickly blanch but don't overcook.

- *Mizuna*, called "pot herb mustard" in English, has long stems and jagged leaves that resemble dandelions. It has a mild taste with a hint of natural acidity. The stems, which you also cook, have a wonderful texture.

- *Shungiku* are the fragrant leaves of a kind of chrysanthemum. This green has a strong, slightly bitter flavor that's distinct in the same way that the flavor of arugula is distinct (although the two are not alike). It's a classic hot pot ingredient that complements bold foods like meat.

Burdock root: This tapered, brown-colored root resembles the business end of a whip, about 3/4 inch at its thickest, and up to 3 feet long. Burdock imparts a sweet, earthy flavor to a broth. It's a mainstay of the rustic hot pots of Japan's far northern snow country and pairs beautifully with meat as well as other roots. Burdock has a hard, woody flesh that usually must be precooked

(see "How to Slice and Poach Burdock Root," page 49). Never peel it, as most of its flavor is found close to its skin. Instead, either lightly scrape off the brown dirt on its surface with the back of a knife or, better, lightly scour it with an all-purpose scrubbing pad under running water to reveal its white flesh (a gentler touch than a knife). Rinse off any excess dirt. Also, if you're not cooking with it immediately, soak burdock in water treated with vinegar as soon as you clean it; otherwise it will oxidize and discolor. Use a teaspoon of distilled white or rice vinegar per cup of water.

Taro: This root, like burdock, is usually found in more rustic hot pots. Japanese taro is about the size of an egg, and has hairy brown skin, which you peel off. Its cream-colored flesh is sweet, earthy, and a touch starchy, with a slightly sticky consistency. Look for firm roots that have unblemished skin.

Tofu: Soybean curd is loaded with protein, and rich in calcium, iron, and vitamins. For our recipes, use Japanese-style or Korean-style tofu, if possible. Both are produced here, are available at Asian markets, and have a more sublime soybean flavor than supermarket varieties do. Tofu comes in many styles, but we use the following four kinds for hot pots.

- *Firm tofu (momen)* can stand up to longer simmering, and is the one we use most often for hot pots.

- *Silken tofu (kinugoshi)* has a delightful, fresh flavor but a very delicate texture, so handle gingerly.

- *Broiled tofu (yakidofu)* is firm tofu that, yes, has been broiled, which reduces moisture, concentrates flavor, and gives the bean curd its distinctive toasty surface, a nice aesthetic highlight. If you can't find broiled tofu, substitute the firm variety, but don't broil it yourself.

Clockwise from top left: *SHUNGIKU*, MIZUNA, AND NAPA CABBAGE

Clockwise from top left: SILKEN TOFU, *ABURA AGE*, BROILED TOFU, AND FIRM TOFU

- *Abura age* (abu-rah ah-geh) is tofu that has been thinly sliced and deep fried. There are a number of *abura age* varieties; for our recipes, use the one shaped like a rectangle about 3 by 6 inches in size and $^1/_4$ inch thick. They usually come several to a pack and can be stored frozen for months. Since it's deep fried, we first "wash" this tofu in boiling water to remove any excess oil.

By the way, you'll notice in the recipes that we usually call for big blocks of tofu (like that glorious bean curd in the cover photograph). Why the hefty hunks? More a Japanese custom than anything else. The outsized pieces look impressive in the pot—and are fun to break apart with chopsticks.

Hot pot noodles: In hot pots, noodles are traditionally eaten two ways—either cooked in the dish from the beginning or added as the *shime* (finish), at the end of the meal. The more familiar Japanese noodles, udon (wheat) and soba (buckwheat), are typically eaten as *shime*, which we'll get to later in this chapter. For cooking, Japanese use a number of less familiar noodles that serve to absorb flavor, add texture, and fill the belly from the get-go. This is economical eating, after all.

- *Harusame* are thin, transparent noodles made from mung bean, potato, or sweet potato starch. They have to be soaked first, and depending on the noodle—they can be up to a foot long—cut in half or thirds before cooking. *Harusame* absorb the flavors of other ingredients and turn the color of the broth as they cook.

- *Itokonnyaku* and *shirataki* are both squiggly, translucent noodles made from *konnyaku*, a gelatin produced from a type of root. *Itokonnyaku* are usually brownish-colored, about the thickness of spaghetti. *Shirataki* noodles are white-colored and thinner.

These noodles don't absorb as much flavor as *harusame*; instead, they're enjoyed more for their pleasing chewy texture.

Developing Flavor

Traditional Japanese flavorings weave together the various foods in a hot pot to create a deliciously complex and balanced composition, even in cooking as simple as these dishes. Balance is the key. You add miso, fermented soybean paste, to mellow a bold ingredient like pork, or mirin, a sweet liquid, to match savory soy sauce. Classic Japanese flavor combinations, which we use throughout the book, always work to reach a harmonious equilibrium. And while the ingredients below may be unfamiliar in name, if you're a fan of sushi you already love their taste—they're fundamental to all Japanese cuisine.

Soy sauce: An essential ingredient in Japanese cuisine, soy sauce adds character, umami-laden savoriness, and caramel flavor and color to foods. In our hot pots, we use two types of Japanese soy sauce, traditionally fermented from soybeans and wheat. We prefer Japanese soy sauces rather than Chinese and other varieties because they are more subtle, and not as strongly fermented. Now, what about tamari? This dark, dense soy sauce, produced from just soybeans, has an intense flavor and is typically used in Japan as a condiment for sashimi or as an ingredient in sauces like teriyaki. We shy away from it for hot pot dishes because it's too overpowering.

- *Koikuchi* is the all-purpose, dark-colored, standard Japanese soy sauce, readily available at Japanese and Asian markets (quality and price vary depending on whether it's produced in volume or is a small-batch, artisanal product). When we call for soy sauce in the recipes, this is the one we mean.

- *Usukuchi* is a lighter soy sauce from the Kansai region (around Kyoto) that we use in more delicate dishes. "Lighter" here means lighter in color, not in taste or saltiness (*usukuchi*, in fact, is saltier than *koikuchi*, a result of its shorter fermentation period). *Usukuchi* adds wonderful flavor and umami to hot pots, but doesn't overwhelm a broth. When we use it in a recipe, we specify it by name.

Sake: The quintessential Japanese alcoholic beverage, sake also plays a central role in cooking. Sake is produced from special rice that has been polished to remove its outer layer, then brewed in a process akin to brewing beer, rather than making wine. (Thus, calling it "rice wine" is a misnomer.) When used to prepare food, it adds singular flavor, delicate sweetness, acidity, depth, and body to dishes, and is vital for mellowing the fishiness in seafood (see "The End of Fishiness," page 73). Some of the sake's alcohol, by the way, evaporates as it simmers. The most important rule here to keep in mind: don't cook with so-called "cooking sake"—a feeble facsimile of the real thing. Always use the actual brew, which is immeasurably more interesting. You don't need the fanciest kind, though. A decent imported *junmai* sake, a basic style, is perfect for cooking (that word is on the label). It costs about twenty dollars for a giant 1.8-liter bottle (about 8 cups), and once opened, can be stored in the refrigerator for up to three months.

Mirin: A fundamental Japanese ingredient, mirin is brewed from glutinous rice (kin to sticky rice from Southeast Asia) to produce a sweet cooking liquid more nuanced than plain sugar. Mirin adds depth, body, its own umami-rich flavor, and an appealing shiny glaze to the foods cooking with it. Mirin is sometimes referred to as "sweet cooking sake" or "sweet sake seasoning." Those are confusing misnomers, as mirin has nothing to do with sake, although it contains alcohol. Most mirin available here is the mass-produced kind, which works fine. But if you can find small-batch, artisanal mirin, which sometimes makes its way to Japanese market

shelves, grab it; the flavor is much deeper. Mirin's alcohol burns off as it cooks.

Japanese salt: Important in Japanese cooking in two ways, salt interacts with the natural umami compounds in foods like dashi to boost their savory impact and is also indispensable for curing fish to concentrate and mellow its flavor. Salt crystals, however, don't form anywhere on land in Japan, so they've long been extracted there from seawater. You can find this traditional salt, called *arajio*, in Japanese markets. Its coarse crystals are still damp with brine and brimming with complex mineral and ocean flavors. Incredible salt. *Arajio* is quite potent, so be careful not to oversalt. At about five dollars for a 1-kilogram bag (2.2 pounds), it's also less expensive than typical gourmet salts. You can also dry *arajio* to make it easier to sprinkle. Just spread it out on a sheet pan and bake at 400°F for 10 minutes. Cool before using.

Miso: Hundreds of varieties of this classic Japanese staple are found across the country, and like wine and cheese, each reflects local customs, their producers, and an ineffable sense of *terroir*. Miso, a paste, is fermented from soybeans and salt, or soybeans, salt, and rice or barley. Look for ones with just these ingredients and no additional additives. Varying in taste from lightly sweet to deeply savory, miso adds robust, umami-laden flavor to other ingredients. It's also a concentrated source of protein and a cultured, living substance like yogurt with lactic acid–forming bacteria that aids digestion. In the recipes, we use the four types described here.

- *Shiro miso* (white miso) refers to the salty, rice-based miso whose savory taste we're most familiar with, the standard ingredient in sushi bar miso soup. Despite its name, its color ranges from straw to yellow ocher. Look for *Shinshu shiro* (*Shinshu white*), a versatile variety from the Japanese Alps

Clockwise from top left: *SHIRATAKI*, POTATO STARCH *HARUSAME*, *ITOKONNYAKU*, AND MUNG BEAN STARCH *HARUSAME*

Clockwise from top left: *SAIKYO* MISO, *SHIRO* MISO, *AKA* MISO, AND *HATCHO* MISO

that is widely available here, or use another salty, rice-based white variety.

- *Aka miso* (red miso) refers to a salty, rice-based miso that's aged longer than white, producing a deeper savory dimension and reddish color. Look for *Sendai* miso, a red miso ground to a coarse paste, which gives it a rustic, farmhouse feeling. Otherwise, *Shinshu aka* (Shinshu red) or other salty, rice-based red varieties work great.

- *Hatcho miso* is a dense, chocolate-hued soybean-and-salt paste with a meaty savoriness. Traditionally fermented in huge cedar barrels for at least two years, *Hatcho* marries perfectly with strong-flavored foods like meat and root vegetables. It's one of our favorites. You can substitute *aka dashi*, which is *Hatcho* cut with *shiro* miso and is sometimes easier to find.

- *Saikyo miso* is the signature cream-colored variety of Kyoto. It has the highest proportion of rice of any miso and is only lightly fermented, which gives it its trademark sweet flavor. *Saikyo* is a very refined miso with a smooth, silky texture, one we use in Kyoto-style hot pots and to add a note of delicate sweetness to other dishes.

Accents and Garnishes

The final flourish to hot pots, Japanese accents and garnishes add even more aroma and dimension to the myriad vibrant flavors already simmering in a dish. You don't cook with these ingredients or they'd lose their potency and alluring fragrance. Instead, sprinkle or dip into them just before eating to tantalize the palate with a hint of heat, spice, or citrusy zip. How much accent and garnish you add depends on your individual taste. As you get to know these ingredients, try different ones with various hot pots, beyond our suggestions in the book.

Sansho: A relative of the Chinese Sichuan pepper (both not true peppers), this ground spice gives off an intense citrus fragrance. More aromatic than hot, *sansho* typically accents rich foods to balance their fattiness.

Shichimi togarashi: This popular Japanese spice made from a mixture of seven ingredients originated in the 1600s. Ground chili is the main component, to which *sansho*, sesame seed, and other aromatics and flavorings like yuzu (a citrus) peel, mustard seed, poppy seed, and hemp seed are added. Different regions, producers, restaurants, and even families claim their own bespoke blends. *Shichimi togarashi* is very versatile, and can accent many different foods.

Momiji oroshi: This lively garnish, made from daikon grated together with dried chilies, has a pleasing red color (hence the evocative *momiji* or "red maple leaf" in the name). Typically paired with a thin sauce like ponzu (see page 20), *momiji oroshi* adds spiciness and heat, but also blends with the liquid to thicken it so it adheres better to foods. You'll find our version on page 35.

Daikon oroshi: If you don't desire the heat of *momiji oroshi*, you can use *daikon oroshi* instead, which is just grated daikon. The spicy tip of the daikon is best for this garnish, which adds the same thickening qualities to ponzu and other thin sauces.

Thinly sliced scallions: Eaten raw as a garnish, scallions cleanse and refresh the palate, bestow an appealing bright green color, and add aroma and a touch of sharpness to balance bold-flavored foods. In Japan, cooks typically use thinly sliced *negi* instead (which you can do, too), but scallions work perfectly, especially when mellowed though a simple technique called *shibori* (see page 43).

Clockwise from top left: RED AND GREEN *YUZU KOSHO*, *SHICHIMI TOGARASHI*, *SHIBORI* SCALLIONS, *SANSHO*, *MITSUBA*, AND *MOMIJI OROSHI*

Ponzu: Savory, sweet, and tart all at once, ponzu is a thin sauce with many applications in Japanese cuisine. Typically a bracing blend of Japanese citrus, soy sauce, and dashi, you can buy it bottled in Japanese and Asian markets. Many varieties are offered for sale; a simple yuzu citrus–based one works great. Even better, you can easily whip up a fragrant ponzu from scratch with lemons, limes, and grapefruit (page 34). Besides hot pots, ponzu is a perfect complement to grilled chicken, meat, and fish, as well as steamed fish and lobster—it's truly versatile.

Yuzu kosho: This zesty accent, in our opinion, is one of Japan's best kept culinary secrets. An alluring, aromatic combination of fiery chilies and tangy Japanese yuzu citrus zest and juice, *yuzu kosho* is available two ways: the more rounded red or the sharper green. Red works best for seafood; green for poultry and meat. Either way, it adds palate-popping flavor to hot pots. *Yuzu kosho* can last for months in the refrigerator, and is an all-purpose accent that also pairs beautifully with grilled chicken, meat, or fish.

Karashi mustard: Ground from a blend of pure mustard seeds, *karashi* isn't cut with vinegar or other additives like your garden-variety, squeeze-bottle type. As a result, it's sinus-clearing potent, so dab gingerly. It's sold as a paste in a tube or in powder form. For the powder, add hot water to work it into a thick paste, wait a minute or two for the heat to come alive, and use. At Japanese markets, it's also called "hot mustard" or "Japanese mustard."

Wasabi: A classic Japanese ingredient, wasabi's fragrance, clean flavor, and subtle heat enliven the palate like nothing else. The bright, lime-colored flesh of this rhizome is sometimes compared to horseradish, but it's considerably less harsh and exceedingly more nuanced. Fresh wasabi is expensive and truly sublime, but is hard to find here. If you can get your hands on it, grate it with a fine grater. The alternatives are pure wasabi paste in a tube, or an economical wasabi-flavored mixture, sold in a tube or as a powder.

Fast Cooking

Hot pots cook very fast; in fact, almost all of the recipes in the book are ready in less than thirty minutes. So why don't they simmer as long as a slow-cooker dish or classic Western stew, which take hours to reach perfection? How these dishes develop flavor makes all the difference. Western stews must slowly tease the essence out of raw ingredients, herbs, and seasonings by simmering over low heat for a long time. Hot pots, on the other hand, like much of Japanese cuisine, rely on fermented and dried ingredients such as miso, soy sauce, and the elements that make up dashi. These foods, if you think about it, are in a sense "precooked;" the process of natural preservation has already formed and released their concentrated flavors. So when added to a hot pot, they rapidly imbue other ingredients with their mouthwatering, satisfying essence—thus, no need for the long haul over heat.

HOT POT COOKWARE

What kind of pot to cook your dish? The two best options: Japanese clay *donabe* (doh-nah-beh), the traditional vessel for most hot pot cooking, or Western-style enameled cast-iron or cast-iron cookware. The difference is in how they react to heat. Use a 4^1/$_2$- to 5-quart (or larger) pot to fit all the ingredients in these recipes.

Japanese clay *donabe*: This vessel's earthenware body evenly conducts and spreads heat across the pot, as clay retains temperature better than any other cookware material. *Donabe* typically have a rounded bottom like a Chinese wok, and a domed lid, both designed to efficiently circulate heat through food. In addition, the lid has a small hole to release steam, which prevents pressure from building up and overflowing the pot, and alerts you when the liquid inside is boiling. These features make *donabe* the ideal vessel to envelop simmering hot pots with steady, uniform heat, inside and out—exactly what they require. The finest ones are handmade with a special clay that has superior insulating properties, extracted from an ancient lakebed in central Japan. (The nearby historic pottery towns of Iga and Shigaraki are renowned for these pots.) But factory-made vessels work great, too, and are readily available at Japanese markets. Be careful when handling *donabe*, which come in a variety of lovely styles and colors. *Donabe* often must be tempered before use (read the instructions), and while they can handle direct heat, they're fragile and will crack if dropped.

Western-style enameled cast-iron and cast-iron cookware: These vessels are excellent alternatives to clay pots, and are a lot sturdier, to boot. Like Japanese *donabe*, they uniformly and efficiently spread heat across the pot and through the foods cooking in it. (Stainless steel pots, by comparison, typically get hottest at the point of contact with a burner, but don't do nearly as good a job circulating heat.) Enameled cast-iron and cast-iron pots heat faster than *donabe*, but they don't retain heat quite as long. Also, since these pots don't have a hole in the lid to let steam escape like *donabe*, be sure to leave the lid open a crack when covering them, to serve this purpose (so if you are using an enameled cast-iron, cast-iron or other Western-style pot, "covered" in the recipes means slightly open).

Finally, you will notice in the book that some recipes recommend a cast-iron skillet. Why? Certain fast-cooking hot pots have traditionally been prepared in a special cast-iron Japanese pan so they heat quickly. A cast-iron skillet or shallow enameled cast-iron pan is a perfect alternative to these hard-to-find vessels.

Other cookware: What if you don't have a *donabe*, enameled cast-iron, or cast-iron cookware? We think these vessels are the ideal, but if you own, say, a stainless steel pot, by all means go ahead and cook your hot pot in it! You can also use a Chinese sand pot, an ovenproof glass casserole, or even that old fondue pot gathering dust in the cabinet—any cookware that can take direct heat works fine. In short, make whatever vessel you like your "hot pot." Remember, this is easy, worry-free cooking, so don't stress over the pot.

Utensils: A ladle and a handheld mesh strainer or slotted spoon are indispensable tools for serving the cooked foods from the pot. Japanese markets often sell specialized serving utensils for hot pots, including a curious ladle with a hole in it and nice-looking, dining table–ready implements. Diners are also encouraged to pluck foods with their chopsticks, of course. When serving, just remember that the first ingredients tasted in a hot pot, by custom, are a sampling of the main vegetables, seafood, poultry, or meat.

Main Ingredients

So far we've focused on the broth, foundation, flavor, and accent ingredients of hot pot cooking; in other words, the supporting cast. But what about the headliners—the vegetables, seafood, poultry, and meat that star in these dishes? The operative word here is: freshness. Since hot pots cook so fast, quality counts even more for the main foods. Buy the best ingredients you can. Also, for fish, keep the skin on or remove, as you wish—we like to leave it on because the skin holds a lot of flavor and adds nice texture. For meat, the hot pot recipes typically call for thinly sliced beef, pork, lamb, or venison, which you can buy already sliced or cut yourself (see "How to Slice Meat for Hot Pot," page 115). Find a great local fish market or butcher for ingredients, or check out our Resources section, page 139, for a listing of seafood, poultry, and meat purveyors that can ship pristine foods to your doorstep.

HOW TO COOK AND ENJOY HOT POT

We created the recipes in this book to yield four hearty servings. With a few exceptions, they are organized in this easy-to-follow progression: prepare ingredients, mix the broth, build the hot pot, and cook it.

Prep. Broth. Build. Cook. Keep this mantra in mind and you can't fail.

Hot pot cooking is quick, flexible, and very forgiving. Think of the recipes as guidelines rather than rigid formulas. We urge you follow the proportions for the broth to achieve the right balance of flavors, but the other hot pot ingredients are a different story. For each of our recipes, we outline their classic foods and related quantities, but it's really up to you. Want, say, more beef? Go ahead and add more beef. Love mushrooms? Double up on them. Hate mushrooms? Well, you get the picture. Feel free to add more or less of any particular ingredient you'd like. In addition, throughout the book we suggest many variations to the recipes to give you even more tasty choices, including totally vegetarian options. We hope you try these, too.

There are two ways to cook hot pots: on the stovetop, which is more familiar here, or at the dining table, the way they most often do it in Japan.

Stovetop cooking: We designed our authentic recipes to be cooked the way we typically do here—that is, on the stovetop. (Shabu-shabu dishes, always cooked tableside, are the exception.) Consider this the "default" method for the book. You can easily halve the recipes or double them, as you desire. If your pot can't comfortably hold all the ingredients or broth, add less; if you overfill, your pot may boil over. Once the dish is ready, carefully transfer it to the dining table. Place the pot on a towel or heat-proof plate. The beauty and sheer pleasure of this style of dining is in presenting an incredible hot pot to friends and family gathered around a table to enjoy it together. Give diners a moment to savor its aroma and the beautiful foods bubbling inside. Ladle the ingredients into small bowls, or ask diners to pluck foods directly from the hot pot and dip into a sauce (our recipes will advise). Eat, and repeat. Keep serving in rounds, as many times as dinnertime bellies can handle.

Tableside cooking: Preparing a hot pot tableside is the quintessential way to enjoy this dish in Japan. For good reason. When you cook at the dining table, you're not just making a meal—you and family and friends are sharing much more than food. It's social, entertaining, and a ton of fun, especially for kids. We love cooking hot pot tableside and hope you give it a try. To do so, you need to set up a portable burner on the dining table. Many of our recipes are ideal for preparing this way; we'll note which ones, and give you some guidelines.

For tableside dining, we recommend a portable gas burner powered by a butane cartridge, which is inexpensive and pumps enough BTUs to keep a pot full of broth and ingredients merrily bubbling away. (Google "portable gas burner" to track one down online.) Portable induction burners (with the appropriate cookware) or good portable electric burners work well, too. Avoid burners fueled by sterno or the like; they don't generate enough heat for hot pot cooking.

The process for cooking tableside is straightforward: Place a pot on the burner, array platters of ingredients around it, pour in the broth, and go to town. Usually the meal's host adds the foundation foods, while individual diners cook the main ingredients themselves, but there are no hard rules. Since this cooking is less structured than the stovetop method, you'll have to use your judgment about which foods to simmer and when they are ready. Just don't put too much into the pot at once and keep the broth on a low simmer. (Check out any of our recipes for shabu-shabu, like Beef Shabu-Shabu on page 117, to get an idea of how this cooking works.)

Cook, eat, cook, eat, enjoying the dish in rounds, a little bit at a time. This flexible style lets you easily riff on the recipes—at one memorable dinner, Tadashi cooked oysters, pork belly, then rib eye in the same incredible hot pot. So feel free to improvise. Finally, keep a pitcher with extra broth handy, and add more liquid as necessary. Dining tableside takes longer than stovetop cooking, but it's definitely worth it.

Cat Hot Pot

No, we're not suggesting you poach your kitty! A clay *donabe* may be the perfect vessel for preparing hot pots, but Japanese felines have their own idea: cleverly repurposing this cookware to create the cat equivalent of a four-poster bed. As pet owners across Japan can attest, something about the bowl shape of a *donabe* makes it irresistible to sleepy kitties. So instead of chucking a cracked or chipped pot, they leave them out for the ole Tiggers in their lives (the pots for cooking stored safely out of feline reach, of course). Adorable photos of this phenomenon have seeped into Japanese popular culture as the subject of books, TV shows, and countless postings online. Google *"neko nabe"* (cat hot pot) and you'll see what we mean.

SHIME (THE FINISH)

To someone Japanese, a hot pot, or any meal for that matter, doesn't seem complete without a serving of rice or noodles. More than side dishes, these starches have traditionally been considered the very core of what you eat—meat, fish, or vegetables are just the highlights. This has to do with rice's long-revered position in this culture, a sensibility that remains powerful even in today's modern Japan. So while there's ample enough food in a typical hot pot to stuff you silly, Japanese still need a helping of rice or noodles to feel totally satisfied. Enter the *shime*.

Shime (she-meh) means "finish," a comforting helping of rice or noodles added to the broth that typically ends a hot pot feast. It's an amazing dish. By the time a hot pot dinner winds down, the various foods leisurely simmering in the broth have infused the liquid with heavenly flavors. These the *shime* magically absorbs. Japanese often swear it's the best part of the meal—they're right.

After each hot pot recipe, we'll suggest the *shime* we think best matches it, but feel free to substitute another, if you prefer. If you still have room in your belly, please give it a try. Strain out any big pieces of food remaining in the broth before preparing the *shime* (little bits of ingredients are fine, though). Also, since the amount of broth remaining at the end of a meal varies, of course, you may have to adjust quantities. Finally, in a few particular recipes we suggest a bowl of rice on the side instead of *shime*. This is by longstanding custom, but basically it is a variation on the same theme. Following are the *shime* dishes—rice and noodles—and the methods for cooking them.

Rice *zosui*: This is basically soupy rice, a *shime* that typically complements thinner, more delicate broths. The technique is simple. For four servings, add 2 cups cooked Japanese short grain rice to the remaining broth in a hot pot. Bring to a boil over medium heat. As soon as the hot pot boils, turn off the heat, mix the contents well, and serve in individual bowls.

Rice *ojiya*: This rice resembles risotto and works best with thicker or miso-based broths. To prepare four servings, add 2 cups cooked Japanese short grain rice to the remaining broth in a hot pot. Place over medium heat, stirring and cooking so the liquid reduces and the rice absorbs the broth. Cook until the rice reaches the consistency of thick porridge. Be careful not to burn it. Serve in individual bowls.

Hot Pot Cooking Tips

- Keep an eye on the heat, adjusting as necessary so the pot is at a steady simmer. A too-vigorous bubbling can cause ingredients to break down.

- Keep an eye on your pot as it cooks. If necessary, press ingredients into the broth as they simmer so they poach uniformly (especially useful for cooking greens). Also, skim off any scum that builds up on the surface of the broth.

- Unless we call for it, don't mix or stir hot pots while they cook. The simmering broth takes care of cooking and flavoring everything.

Clockwise from top left: RICE *OJIYA*, *YAKI UDON*, UDON IN BROTH, AND RICE *ZOSUI*

Gorgeous Hot Pots

Stovetop or tableside, either way your hot pot's got to look good. Japanese cooking is as much a feast for the eye as it is for the palate: one of the true joys of a Japanese meal is its simple yet seductive beauty. This goes for fine cuisines like *kaiseki* and sushi, but it also counts in down-home hot pot cooking, albeit in a more relaxed way. Start with a great pot, one that matches the mood of your food. As the photos in the book can attest, there are plenty of alluring choices, both Japanese and Western style. With the most rustic dishes, those born deep in the Japanese countryside, just pile ingredients into a pot and simmer; the shapes and colors of the foods will lend their own rough-hewn grace. (These are always cooked stovetop, as you'll see in the recipes.) With more refined hot pots (but not *too* refined), arrange ingredients in separate, neat bunches, a simple but elegant touch that accentuates their vibrant qualities. Also, we often lay *harusame* or napa cabbage on the bottom of a pot to act as a pedestal, propping up the other foods to highlight them as they simmer. Besides producing arresting dishes, this orderly hot pot organizing also yields a practical result: it helps you find individual foods later in a meal, when the pot inevitably becomes, well, a tad disheveled. Check out our photo sequence on page 90 which shows how to create a gorgeous, mouthwatering hot pot.

You can swirl in raw eggs to either rice dish just before removing from the heat to add more richness and flavor (swirl slowly). People often do this in Japan; the eggs set in the hot rice. Garnish, if you desire, with chopped *mitsuba* (an aromatic Japanese herb), chopped *ohba* leaves (an aromatic herb), shredded nori (papery dried seaweed sheets), or *shibori* scallions (page 43). Finally, you can always start by cooking rice *zosui*, sampling it, then simmering more until it reduces to rice *ojiya*—two-for-one *shime*.

Noodles: We use a variety of Japanese noodles for *shime*:

- *Soba* is a thin buckwheat noodle.

- *Udon, Inaniwa udon* (a variety from the north), and *somen* are types of wheat noodles that vary in thickness.

- *Ramen* is a wheat noodle kneaded with egg.

Soba and udon are often sold precooked, either frozen or refrigerated, and portioned into individual servings (blocks about 1/2 pound each). Use about 1/2 pound (one block) of udon or soba for four servings. Add them to the remaining broth in a hot pot, and bring to a boil over medium heat. As soon as the hot pot boils, turn off the heat and serve the noodles and broth in individual bowls. If you can't find the precooked noodles, use dry noodles instead. Somen and Inaniwa udon are always sold dry. Ramen is also sold dry, but note that it's usually called *chuka soba* or *chukamen* (Chinese noodles) on the package, a testament to its Chinese origin. For all the dry noodles, use 4 ounces for four servings, cooking ahead of time following package instructions. Add them to the remaining broth and ingredients in the hot pot and follow the directions above. (You can also substitute Italian capellini or vermicelli for ramen.)

Yaki udon here refers to noodles braised in a thick broth. Use either 1/2 pound of precooked udon (one block) or 4 ounces of dried udon cooked following package instructions. Add the noodles to the remaining broth in a hot pot. Place over medium heat, cooking and stirring until the broth reduces to a thick gravy. Be careful not to burn. Serve with the gravy in individual bowls.

Mochi: These are dense, unsweetened, white-colored cakes made from pounded glutinous (sticky) rice, usually shaped into either 2-inch-long rectangles or 1 1/2-inch diameter rounds. They're sold hard as stone but turn delightfully pillowy when cooked. Use two per person (more, if your appetite is hearty). Add the mochi to the remaining broth in a hot pot. Bring to a boil over medium heat. As soon as the hot pot boils, turn off the heat and serve the mochi and broth in individual bowls.

EVERY HOT POT HAS A STORY

We've covered everything you need to know to make this food; now the fun part begins. In the pages that follow, you'll discover our favorite hot pots, authentic dishes we've savored all across Japan with friends, families, farmers, fishermen, cops, even beefy sumo wrestlers.

These hot pots are more than just recipes, they're the very soul food of this country. Travel through Japan and you'll find them everywhere, from the miso-and-salmon variety of the far north to the chicken-and-mushroom dish of the deep south. In between, you'll taste veggie, tofu, tuna, cod, crab, shrimp, duck, beef, pork, venison, wild boar, even city slicker–style hamburger hot pots—almost every food eaten there finds its way into this chow.

As you'll soon see, each one of these wholesome, comforting dishes tells a story. About the culture. About regional food. About how to cook Japanese. And most important, about the people.

Japanese Rice

Always use Japanese-style short grain rice for *shime*. Some of the best in the world is grown in California, so it's widely available here. Japanese typically cook with white rice (both the bran and nutritious germ removed). What about brown rice? Brown doesn't readily absorb the flavorful broth as well, because of its tough bran, and its nutty taste can overpower, but if you love brown rice, enjoy! Another option is *haigamai* or *haiga* rice, available at Japanese markets, and also domestically produced. With this rice, the bran is removed but not the germ. So *haiga* drinks in flavor, is more nutritious than white, but doesn't tend to overwhelm like brown. Cook it just like white rice (see page 36).

Hot Pots Online

Got questions about hot pot cooking, ingredients, and techniques? We've created a website to help you out: **www.japanesehotpots.com**. It's packed with information, how-to videos, even links for buying authentic Japanese clay *donabe*.

Hot pots trace their roots to ancient times, when the charcoal-burning hearth was the centerpiece of the Japanese home. Families gathered around this nurturing fire to prepare their meals, eat, and share stories. Fast forward to today: the hearth may be gone but the sensibility endures. Japanese have long believed that sharing a meal from a single pot forges closer relationships. Amen to that.

Once you enjoy hot pots with family and friends, you'll understand why a portable burner and clay pot can be found in practically every cupboard of every Japanese home. Japanese cherish their beloved hot pots, and we hope you will, too.

BASIC RECIPES

DASHI

Kombu-Katsuobushi Dashi

This is a foolproof recipe for an all-purpose dashi made with kombu and dried, shaved bonito that we cook with throughout the book. Use it hot off the stove, cold out of the fridge, or at room temperature. You can prepare dashi 3 days ahead of time and store in the refrigerator, or store in the freezer for up to 2 months. If you're pressed for time, you can also make dashi with store-bought "dashi packs." These look like giant teabags that you simply stick in water and heat (follow package instructions), and are available in Japanese markets. Although all-natural, they're not nearly as good as the real thing. Finally, avoid "dashi powder" (or hon dashi), another option, but one filled with additives.

MAKES ABOUT 6 CUPS

8 cups water, plus 2 tablespoons water

2 (6-inch) pieces kombu

1½ ounces dried, shaved bonito (about 3 packed cups)

Add the 8 cups of water and the kombu to a large stockpot and let it steep for 30 minutes.

Place the stockpot over medium heat and bring it to a boil. Remove the kombu. Add the remaining 2 tablespoons of water. Add the bonito and stir it once to mix in. As soon as the liquid boils again, decrease the heat to low and simmer for 5 minutes. Remove any scum that appears on the surface; it can affect flavor.

Turn off the heat and let the liquid steep for 15 minutes. Strain the liquid through a fine sieve or cheesecloth. Don't squeeze the bonito flakes. Discard the bonito flakes after using.

JAPANESE CHICKEN STOCK
Tori Gara Dashi

Japanese chicken stock is made from just bones and water; the roots and herbs that typically enhance the Western version aren't used. The concept is to create pure chicken flavor that can be layered with other ingredients simmering in it (like the ingredients in hot pots). You can refrigerate this stock for up to 5 days, so it's easy to make ahead of time.

MAKES ABOUT 8 CUPS

1 pound chicken bones and wings (roughly chop the ribcage, if using)

12 cups water, plus more for boiling the bones

Place the chicken bones in a large stockpot, fill it with enough water to cover, and bring to a boil over high heat. Remove from the heat. Strain the bones and discard the water. (Pouring off the boiled water will remove blood and coagulated proteins, which can cloud the stock's flavor.) Rinse the bones under running water to wash off any scum.

Return the bones to the pot. Add the 12 cups water and bring the pot to a boil over high heat. Decrease the heat to medium and simmer until the stock reduces to approximately 8 cups, about 30 minutes. As it cooks, check the stock at regular intervals to remove any scum that appears on the surface. Strain the liquid and discard the bones.

NAPA CABBAGE-SPINACH ROLLS

Hakusai Maki

Besides adding a playful and aesthetically pleasing touch to hot pots, these rolls have practical benefits, too: they're compact, precooked, and won't dilute a broth, since the liquid in the napa cabbage and spinach has already been released by blanching (a desirable thing for some hot pots). The rolls should be about $1^1/_2$ inches in diameter. To make them, you'll need a bamboo sushi mat, which can be found in any Asian market.

MAKES 1 ROLL

4 ounces napa cabbage leaves, separated from the head (about 4 large leaves)

4 ounces spinach, stemmed

Bring a large pot of water to a boil over high heat. Trim the hard white stems from the cabbage leaves (add them to a hot pot if you'd like). Blanch the leaves in the boiling water until they soften, about 30 seconds. Transfer the cabbage to a colander, reserving the cooking water, and rinse under running water until the leaves are cool. Gently squeeze out any excess liquid from the leaves with your hands; reserve.

Add the spinach to the boiling water and quickly blanch it until it cooks through, about 30 seconds. Transfer the spinach to a colander and rinse under running water until it cools. Gently squeeze out any excess liquid from the leaves; reserve.

Spread a single layer of the cabbage leaves over a bamboo sushi mat, laying the leaves top to bottom, one next to the other, overlapping by up to one-third of a leaf. Place a row of spinach lengthwise in the center of the mat, over the cabbage. Starting at the bottom edge, roll the sushi mat to create a cylinder of cabbage leaves with the bright green spinach in the middle. Make sure to roll the mat tightly so the leaves don't fall apart while cooking. Squeeze the rolled mat over the sink to remove any excess liquid.

Remove the sushi mat and tightly wrap the roll with plastic wrap, to make cutting easier. Slice the cylinder into 4 pieces, each about 2 inches wide. Remove the plastic wrap before using.

PONZU

You can find a variety of bottled ponzu in Japanese markets, but nothing beats making it fresh. Always use a combination of different citrus to prepare ponzu. Fresh yuzu and sudachi, types of Japanese citrus, are classic ponzu ingredients (if you can find them), but lemons, limes, and grapefruit work great, too. This sauce will keep in the refrigerator for up to 2 weeks.

MAKES ABOUT 1 1/2 CUPS

2 tablespoons mirin

1/2 cup dashi (page 30)

1/2 cup freshly squeezed citrus juice
(any combination of lemon, lime, grapefruit,
yuzu, or sudachi)

1/4 cup soy sauce

2 tablespoons usukuchi soy sauce (page 14)

Add the mirin to a small saucepan and bring it to a boil over medium heat. Remove from the heat and let it cool to room temperature. Combine the mirin with the dashi, juice, and both soy sauces, mixing well. You can use the ponzu immediately, or, better, cover and refrigerate for 8 to 12 hours to give it more time for the flavors to mingle. Serve at room temperature.

VARIATION: You can make ponzu totally vegetarian by substituting mushroom stock (see Kabocha Pumpkin Hot Pot, page 47, for our recipe) for the dashi.

MOMIJI OROSHI

While Japanese markets sell bottled *momiji oroshi kobin* (red pepper paste for *momiji oroshi*) to mix with grated daikon to produce this condiment, we prefer making it from scratch, which tastes better and avoids the additives in the bottled version. The Japanese dried chilies used here are called *togarashi*. There are two ways to make *momiji oroshi*: the age-old original way or the short-cut way. Here's the old-school recipe.

MAKES ABOUT ¹/₄ CUP

8 whole dried Japanese chilies

¹/₂ pound daikon, peeled and quartered lengthwise (the zesty tip or mellower middle of the root works best)

Soak the chilies in hot water for 5 minutes. Use the bottom of a chopstick to poke a hole into the flat end of one piece of the daikon. Stuff a chili into the hole, using the chopstick as a plunger (a Japanese chili is about the same diameter as a chopstick).

Grate the two together with a fine grater. When you've used up the chili, poke another hole in the daikon, stick in another chili, and continue grating. Repeat for the remaining pieces of daikon.

Mix the rose-colored grated daikon well and squeeze out any extra liquid.

VARIATION: You can simply mix ¹/₄ cup grated daikon (extra liquid squeezed off) with ¹/₂ teaspoon red *yuzu kosho* (page 20) to produce a fresh-tasting similar result. The flavor will be different (*yuzu kosho* adds citrus notes) but faster and convenient, and it makes a totally acceptable version that we use, too.

JAPANESE RICE FOR SHIME

Gohan

Two basic ways to prepare Japanese rice: rice cooker or stovetop. If you have an electric rice cooker, wash and rest the rice as we describe below, then follow cooker instructions. To prepare rice on the stovetop, a Japanese clay *donabe* (see page 21) or Western-style enameled cast-iron or cast-iron pot works best. You can make rice for *shime* up to 3 days ahead of time and store in the fridge until you're ready.

MAKES 4 CUPS

2 cups Japanese short grain white or haiga rice (page 27)

2 cups water, plus more for washing rice

Wash the rice to remove surface starch by placing the rice in a bowl, filling it with water, and swirling the rice with your hand while at the same time gently rubbing grains together with your fingers. Drain off the milky liquid. Repeat 2 or 3 times until the water becomes clear enough to see the rice. Wash quickly; the entire process should take no longer than 3 minutes. (Soaking the rice in the washing water too long can cloud its flavor.)

Transfer the rice to a colander, cover with a clean kitchen towel, and let it rest for 15 minutes so the grains naturally rehydrate, which helps them cook evenly.

Add the rice and the 2 cups of water to a pot. Cover and bring to a boil over high heat. (With a Western-style pot, keep the cover slightly open to tell when the water boils, then cover fully for the next step.) Decrease the heat to medium and cook until you smell a beautiful rice aroma in the steam escaping from the pot, about 10 minutes. Be careful not to overcook or you'll burn the rice.

Remove from the heat and let the fully covered pot sit for 10 minutes, a critical step that completes the cooking process.

Uncover the pot, gently stir the rice with a large spoon to fluff it up, and it's ready. The rice may have a toasted crust on the bottom, which is considered a delicacy in Japan called *okoge*. If you find this crunchy, caramelized crust, be sure to enjoy it, too.

VEGETABLES AND TOFU

MUSHROOM HOT POT
Kinoko Nabe

This hot pot hails from Japan's far northern snow country where, every autumn, mushroom pickers comb the region's rugged mountains to forage for wild *maitake*, *shimeji*, and *nameko*. And every autumn, families there enjoy this flavorful hot pot to mark the start of the cold season. We use a mixture of cultivated Japanese mushrooms in the recipe, but you can add any kind you'd like, including fresh wild mushrooms such as chanterelles, trumpets, and porcini.

SERVES 4

4 cups dashi (page 30)

1 cup sake

1/2 cup mirin

1/2 cup soy sauce

1/2 pound napa cabbage, sliced (page 52)

1/2 package (about 1/2 pound) firm tofu, cut into 4 pieces

1/2 pound shiitake mushrooms (about 16 pieces), stemmed

1/2 pound oyster mushrooms, trimmed and pulled apart

3 1/2 ounces (100-gram package) shimeji mushrooms, trimmed and pulled apart

7 ounces (200-gram package) enoki mushrooms, trimmed and pulled apart

1/2 pound spinach, stemmed

Shichimi togarashi (page 18), for accent

Prepare the broth by combining the dashi, sake, mirin, and soy sauce in a bowl; reserve.

Add the cabbage and tofu to a hot pot and pour in the broth. Cover the pot and bring it to a boil over high heat. Decrease the heat to medium and simmer for 5 minutes more.

Uncover the hot pot and add the shiitake mushrooms, oyster mushrooms, *shimeji* mushrooms, and enoki mushrooms, piling them randomly on top of the other ingredients. Cover the pot and simmer for 5 minutes more. Uncover the pot, add the spinach, and simmer for 1 minute more.

Transfer the hot pot to the dining table. Serve the ingredients together with the broth, accenting with *shichimi togarashi*.

Suggested shime: *Soba (page 26).*

VARIATION: To prepare this hot pot totally vegetarian, substitute mushroom stock (see Kabocha Pumpkin Hot Pot, page 47, for our recipe) for the dashi. This vegetarian stock will yield 8 tasty reconstituted shiitake mushrooms, which you can substitute for half of the fresh shiitake in the recipe (remove their stems before cooking).

"NEEDLE" HOT POT

Hari Hari Nabe

This delicious hot pot is utterly simple to prepare, with just two main ingredients: mizuna greens and *abura age* (deep-fried tofu cakes). The "needle" in the name refers to the pointy edges of the fresh-tasting mizuna. This dish, interestingly, originated in the whaling ports of central Japan and was originally cooked with whale meat instead of tofu.

SERVES 4

8 abura age cakes (page 14)

4 cups dashi (page 30)

1 cup mirin

1/2 cup soy sauce

3/4 pound mizuna, trimmed and stems cut into 2-inch pieces

1/4 cup daikon oroshi (page 18), for garnish

Sansho (page 18), for accent

Fill a saucepan with water and bring it to a boil over high heat. Decrease the heat to medium and add the *abura age*. Boil for 1 minute to remove the excess oil from its surface. Strain the *abura age* and cut each piece in half. Set aside.

Prepare the broth by combining the dashi, mirin, and soy sauce in a bowl.

Place the *abura age* in a hot pot and pour in the broth. Cover the hot pot and bring it to a boil over high heat. Decrease the heat to medium and simmer for 10 minutes. Uncover the pot and add the mizuna. Cover the pot and cook for another 5 minutes.

Transfer the hot pot to the dining table. Serve the ingredients together with the broth in small bowls. Garnish with the *daikon oroshi* and accent with *sansho*.

Suggested shime: *Udon (page 26).*

VARIATION: To prepare this hot pot totally vegetarian, substitute mushroom stock (see Kabocha Pumpkin Hot Pot, page 47, for our recipe) for the dashi.

KYOTO VEGETABLE HOT POT

Kyo-Yasai Nabe

Our friend Mr. Hisao Nakahigashi inspired this recipe. A revered Kyoto chef, Mr. Nakahigashi prepares this homey dish as a staff meal, using the leftover peels, pieces, and stems of the heirloom vegetables he serves his customers ("don't waste" being a core Japanese cooking maxim). Called *kyo-yasai*, these traditional vegetables are unique to the urban farms that dot the city and are protected by law. We loved this hot pot when we first tasted it at his restaurant, and now we cook this totally vegetarian dish in our homes with ingredients we find here. The versatile cutting style we use to slice the burdock is called *rangiri*, a simple technique to shape certain roots to uniform size so they cook evenly, one we employ throughout the book.

SERVES 4

6 ounces burdock root, cleaned (page 11)

6 ounces lotus root, peeled, halved lengthwise, and cut into 1/4-inch-thick slices

1 1/2 medium carrots (about 6 ounces), peeled

2 (6-inch) pieces kombu

3 small taro roots (about 1/2 pound), peeled and quartered lengthwise (cut quarters in half if more than 2 inches long)

1/2 pound daikon, peeled, quartered lengthwise, and cut into 1/4-inch-thick slices

4 cups water, plus more for cooking

3/4 cup saikyo miso (page 18)

1 tablespoon shiro miso (page 15)

4 ounces shiitake mushrooms (about 8 pieces), stemmed

3 1/2 ounces (100-gram package) shimeji mushrooms, trimmed and pulled apart

4 ounces mizuna, trimmed and stems cut into 2-inch pieces

Shichimi togarashi (page 18), for accent

Slice the burdock root into 2-inch pieces by cutting on an angle and rolling the root a quarter turn after each slice.

Add the burdock and lotus roots to a small saucepan and cover with water. Bring to a boil over high heat. Decrease the heat to medium and simmer until the roots become tender, about 20 minutes. Strain and set aside.

Cut the carrots into 2-inch pieces by cutting on an angle and rolling the carrot a quarter turn after each slice.

Place the kombu on the bottom of a hot pot and add the carrots, taro roots, and daikon in a random pile over it.

Add the 4 cups of water. Cover the pot and bring it to a boil over high heat. Decrease the heat to medium and simmer for 10 minutes.

Uncover the pot and remove the kombu. Add the reserved burdock and lotus roots. Place the *saikyo* and *shiro* misos in a wire mesh strainer, submerge the strainer into the hot pot liquid, and stir the miso with chopsticks until it dissolves. Add the shiitake mushrooms and *shimeji* mushrooms and simmer for 5 minutes. Add the mizuna and simmer for 2 minutes more.

Transfer the hot pot to the dining table. Serve the ingredients together with the broth in small bowls. Accent with *shichimi togarashi*.

Suggested side dish: *Individual bowls of steamed rice.*

VARIATIONS: You can add about ½ pound of uncooked shucked oysters, scallops, sliced chicken, or sliced pork belly to this hot pot, too, if you'd like. These ingredients pair nicely with the natural sweetness of the *saikyo* miso and the root vegetables. Add the chicken with the carrots, taro roots, and daikon; the other ingredients with the burdock and lotus roots.

Shibori Scallions

Raw scallions (green onions) add fragrance and flavor to dishes, but their sharpness can overwhelm other foods. So we use a traditional technique called *shibori* to cut the scallions' bite and make them milder, while still preserving their taste. Slice 2 ounces of trimmed scallions into thin rings, both the white and green parts. Fill a bowl with water and add the scallion slices. Soak them for 10 minutes. With a slotted spoon, transfer the scallions to a clean kitchen towel and wring the towel over the sink to squeeze out excess moisture (and any sliminess). After wringing the scallions, mix them well. *Shibori* scallions can keep in the refrigerator for up to 3 days. Makes ½ cup.

TOFU HOT POT

Yudōfu

Kyoto, the ancient capital of Japan, is the birthplace of *shojin ryori*, the traditional Buddhist vegetarian cuisine eaten at the city's numerous temples. Tofu is a mainstay of this cooking, and to this day, artisanal tofu makers in Kyoto can be found preparing fresh bean curd every morning before dawn. Tofu hot pot is a classic dish of this city, especially in the winter. Make sure to handle the delicate silken tofu carefully so it doesn't crumble. Also, the broth here is just a cooking liquid rather than served with ingredients (but it's great for *shime*). *Warijoyu*, made from soy sauce mellowed by dashi and sweet mirin, is a versatile condiment that can also complement steamed asparagus, spinach, broccoli, or steamed flounder. For vegetarians, substitute straight soy sauce for the *warijoyu* (to avoid the fish in the dashi).

SERVES 4

WARIJOYU

1/2 cup soy sauce

1/4 cup dashi (page 30)

2 tablespoons mirin

—

2 (6-inch) pieces kombu

2 packages (about 1 pound each) silken tofu, each cut into 6 blocks

4 ounces shiitake mushrooms (about 8 pieces), stemmed, caps halved

1 negi (page 10), sliced on an angle into 2-inch pieces

4 ounces napa cabbage, sliced (page 52)

8 cups water

Shichimi togarashi (page 18), for accent

1/2 cup shibori scallions (page 43), for garnish

To prepare the *warijoyu*, combine the soy sauce, dashi, and mirin in a small saucepan, and bring to a boil over high heat. Remove from the heat and let the liquid cool to room temperature.

Place the kombu on the bottom of a hot pot, then carefully place the tofu over it, in the center. Arrange the shiitake mushrooms, *negi*, and cabbage around the tofu. Add the 8 cups of water.

Cover the pot and bring it to a boil over medium heat. Decrease the heat to low, uncover the pot, and gently simmer until the tofu is warmed through, about 10 minutes. Check at regular intervals to make sure the liquid is not simmering too strongly, which can break apart the tofu.

Transfer the hot pot to the dining table. Serve the ingredients (without the broth) in small bowls, drizzling the *warijoyu* and accenting with *shichimi togarashi*. Garnish with the scallions. Add more *warijoyu*, as desired.

Suggested shime: *Rice* zosui *(page 24). Add any* warijoyu *and* shibori *scallions that remain to the rice.*

TABLESIDE COOKING OPTION: Begin at the dining table after you prepare the *warijoyu*. Cook all the ingredients together as described above. The tofu looks majestic simmering tableside.

KABOCHA PUMPKIN HOT POT
Hōtō Nabe

Kabocha are squat, green pumpkins with orange flesh that resemble sweet potatoes in texture and naturally sweet flavor. Their peak season is around Halloween time, and Japanese enjoy this hot pot to herald the arrival of crisp autumn weather. Look for kabocha that are firm to the touch with dull-colored skin. Be careful when you cut through their tough shells; make sure to use a heavy knife. The skin is edible, but some people prefer to trim most of it away, just leaving a little of the green for color. Kabocha will break down as it simmers, thickening and flavoring the broth in the process. In Japan, this hot pot is typically cooked with special flat noodles that resemble fettuccine, but we use udon instead. The frozen or refrigerated precooked form of udon works best (just drop the blocks into the hot pot), but if you can only find dry udon, cook it following package instructions and rinse well before adding it to the dish.

SERVES 4

MUSHROOM STOCK

8 pieces dried shiitake mushrooms

5 cups water

—

1/2 cup soy sauce

1/2 cup mirin

2 (6-inch) pieces kombu

1/2 kabocha pumpkin (about 1 pound), seeded and cut into bite-size pieces

4 ounces daikon, peeled, halved lengthwise, and cut into 1/2-inch-thick slices

3 small taro roots (about 1/2 pound), peeled and quartered lengthwise (cut quarters in half if more than 2 inches long)

1 medium carrot (about 4 ounces), peeled, halved lengthwise, and cut into 1/2-inch-thick slices

1 negi (page 10), sliced on an angle into 2-inch pieces

4 ounces napa cabbage, sliced (page 52)

3 1/2 ounces (100-gram package) shimeji mushrooms, trimmed and pulled apart

1 pound (2 blocks) frozen, precooked udon noodles, or 8 ounces dried

Shichimi togarashi (page 18), for accent

To make the mushroom stock, combine the dried shiitake mushrooms and the 5 cups of water in a bowl, cover, and steep at room temperature for at least 5 hours. You can make this stock a day ahead of time. (Or, if you're pressed for time, you can steep for just 1 hour, but the longer steep produces a much deeper flavor.)

When the mushroom stock is ready, strain the liquid and reserve both the stock and the reconstituted shiitake mushrooms. Remove and discard the mushroom stems and halve the caps. Set aside.

Prepare the broth by combining the reserved mushroom stock, soy sauce, and mirin in a bowl.

Place the kombu on the bottom of a hot pot and pile the pumpkin, daikon, taro, carrot, *negi*, cabbage, *shimeji*

continued

mushrooms, and reserved shiitake mushrooms over it. Pour in the broth.

Cover the hot pot and bring it to a boil over high heat. Decrease the heat to medium and simmer for 10 minutes. Uncover the pot and add the udon noodles. Simmer until the noodles are tender, about 10 minutes more.

Transfer the hot pot to the dining table. Serve the ingredients together with the broth, accenting with *shichimi togarashi*.

VARIATIONS: You can add uncooked sliced chicken or pork belly to this hot pot, too, if you'd like (add about ¹⁄₂ pound with the pumpkin and other ingredients).

RUSTIC SOBA NOODLE HOT POT
Soba Kakke Nabe

The handmade buckwheat pasta used here is the rustic country cousin of Japan's refined soba noodles and originated in the farmhouses of Aomori Prefecture, a rugged, sparsely populated area located deep in Japan's snow country. Buckwheat (*soba*, in Japanese) is an ideal crop for this region, as it thrives in mountainous soil too poor to support rice or grains. *Kakke* means "broken pieces," which gives you a hint about how to make these noodles—they don't have to look perfect. Be careful not to overcook them, though; they should be prepared just al dente. (Test as they cook by breaking off a little piece with chopsticks, and tasting.) The garlic-miso dip adds a flavorful contrast to the noodles, but if the garlic is too strong for you, you can substitute finely chopped *negi*.

SERVES 4

SOBA DOUGH
1 cup soba flour (fine buckwheat flour), plus more for dusting

¹⁄₄ cup all-purpose flour

1 cup boiling water

MISO DIPPING SAUCE
¹⁄₂ cup aka miso (page 18)

2 cloves garlic, finely chopped or crushed

1 tablespoon sake

1 tablespoon sugar

—

1 medium carrot (about 4 ounces), peeled, halved lengthwise, and cut into ¹⁄₄-inch-thick slices

4 ounces daikon, peeled, quartered lengthwise, and cut into ¹⁄₄-inch-thick slices

2 (6-inch) pieces kombu

¹⁄₄ pound burdock root, sliced and poached (opposite)

¹⁄₂ package (about ¹⁄₂ pound) firm tofu, cut into 4 pieces

1 negi (page 10), sliced on an angle into 2-inch pieces

8 cups water, plus more for cooking vegetables

To prepare the soba dough, place the soba flour, all-purpose flour, and boiling water in a bowl and combine until a dough forms. Lightly dust a work surface with additional soba flour. Knead the dough, dusting it with more soba flour as needed, so it doesn't stick to the surface. After about 5 minutes, the dough should feel elastic to the touch. Form it into a ball and return the dough to the bowl. Cover the bowl with a damp towel and let rest for 30 minutes.

Meanwhile, to make the miso dipping sauce, combine the miso, garlic, sake, and sugar in a bowl, whisking to blend well. Fill four small bowls with the miso sauce. Set aside.

While the dough is resting, add the carrot and daikon to a small saucepan and cover with water. Bring to a boil over high heat. Decrease the heat to medium and simmer for 10 minutes. Strain, discard the cooking water, and set the vegetables aside.

Once the dough has rested, dust the kneading surface with soba flour. With a rolling pin, roll out the dough to $1/8$ inch thick. Divide it into 3-inch strips, then cut triangles out of the strips (about 2 inches wide at the base). Arrange the soba triangles on a platter. Set aside.

Place the kombu on the bottom of a hot pot, and pile the burdock, carrot, daikon, tofu, and *negi* over it. Add the 8 cups of water.

Cover the hot pot and bring it to a boil over high heat. Decrease the heat to medium and simmer for 10 minutes. Uncover the pot and gently layer the soba triangles over the other ingredients. Simmer the soba until the triangles are cooked through, about 5 minutes. As they cook, use chopsticks at regular intervals to separate the triangles.

Transfer the hot pot to the dining table. Dip the ingredients into the miso dipping sauce, and eat. Add more dipping sauce to the bowls, as desired.

TABLESIDE COOKING OPTION: Begin at the dining table by adding the ingredients to the hot pot. Cook the supporting ingredients all at once, or reserve half or more to prepare later. Simmer the rustic soba noodles like a shabu-shabu dish, a little at a time (page 63).

How to Slice and Poach Burdock Root

Clean the burdock as described in the Basics (page 11). Slice it into 2-inch pieces by cutting on an angle and rolling the root a quarter turn after each slice. Add the burdock to a small saucepan and cover with water. Bring to a boil over high heat. Decrease the heat to medium and simmer for 15 minutes. Strain and set aside.

HAND-PULLED NOODLE HOT POT
Hittsumi Nabe

Like Rustic Soba Noodle Hot Pot (page 48), this dish also features handmade, farmhouse pasta from Japan's far northern snow country, but made from wheat rather than buckwheat. This hot pot, though, isn't just found in the countryside. Tadashi's mother regularly prepared this comforting and economical dish when he was growing up in Tokyo. Make sure to cook the noodles thoroughly; they should be soft and pliant when done. You can also prepare the pasta a couple hours ahead of time (up to precooking them). Just store the noodles, loosely covered, in the refrigerator until you're ready to use.

SERVES 4

MUSHROOM STOCK

8 pieces dried shiitake mushrooms

5 cups water

DOUGH

2¼ cups all-purpose flour, plus more for dusting

¼ teaspoon salt

½ cup water, plus more as needed

—

3 tablespoons sake

1 tablespoon mirin

2 tablespoons usukuchi soy sauce (page 14)

½ teaspoon salt

2 (6-inch) pieces kombu

¼ pound burdock root, sliced and poached (page 49)

½ medium carrot (about 2 ounces), peeled, cut into 2-inch pieces, and sliced thin lengthwise

¼ pound napa cabbage, sliced (page 52)

1 negi (page 10), sliced on an angle into 2-inch pieces

3½ ounces (100-gram package) shimeji mushrooms, trimmed and pulled apart

Shichimi togarashi (page 18), for accent

To make the mushroom stock, combine the dried shiitake mushrooms and the 5 cups of water in a bowl, cover, and steep at room temperature for at least 5 hours. You can make this stock a day ahead of time. (Or, if you're pressed for time, you can steep for just 1 hour, but the longer steep produces a much deeper flavor.)

Meanwhile, to prepare the dough, place the flour, salt, and the ½ cup water in a bowl, and combine until a dough forms. (Add 1 or 2 more tablespoons of water if necessary.) Lightly dust a work surface with flour. Knead the dough, dusting it with more flour, as needed, so it

doesn't stick to the surface. After about 5 minutes, the dough should feel elastic to the touch. Form it into a ball and return the dough to the bowl. Cover the bowl with a damp towel and let the dough rest for 1 hour.

Once the dough has rested, fill a saucepan with water and bring it to a boil over medium heat. Meanwhile, pull off small pieces of dough with your fingers, stretching and patting them to form coarsely shaped, 2-inch-round flat noodles. Repeat until you've used all the dough.

continued

When the water boils, add the dough pieces, and cook for 3 minutes. Strain the noodles in a colander and rinse under running water. Set aside.

When the mushroom stock is ready, strain the liquid and reserve both the stock and the reconstituted shiitake mushrooms. Remove and discard the mushroom stems and halve the caps. Set aside.

Prepare the broth by combining the reserved mushroom stock and the sake, mirin, soy sauce, and salt in a bowl; reserve.

Place the kombu on the bottom of a hot pot, and randomly pile the burdock, carrot, cabbage, *negi*, *shimeji* mushrooms, and the reserved shiitake mushrooms over it. Pour in the reserved broth.

Cover the hot pot and bring it to a boil over high heat. Decrease the heat to medium and simmer for 5 minutes. Uncover the pot and add the noodles. Cover the pot again and simmer until the noodles are cooked through and tender, 5 to 10 minutes. (Check the noodles for doneness after 5 minutes.)

Transfer the hot pot to the dining table. Serve the ingredients together with the broth in small bowls, accenting with the *shichimi togarashi*.

VARIATION: In Japan's snow country, chicken is often included in this hot pot. Add $1/2$ pound of chicken with the burdock and other ingredients.

How to Slice Napa Cabbage

Here's the Japanese method for cutting napa cabbage, which helps it to better absorb flavor. Alternatively, you can simply chop it into bite-size pieces; it's up to you. To slice Japanese-style: Trim off the bottom of a head of napa cabbage, separate the leaves, and rinse well to remove any dirt, especially at the stems. Pat them dry. Place a cabbage leaf flat on a cutting board. Starting from the white stem end, cut the leaf on a sharp diagonal into 2-inch-wide pieces. (Cutting on an angle exposes more surface area for the leaf to absorb broth.) Cut the green part of the leaf further, in half or thirds, to make bite-size pieces. Repeat with the remaining leaves.

FISH AND OTHER SEAFOOD

SALMON HOT POT

Ishikari Nabe

Like in Alaska, salmon is a way of life on Hokkaido, Japan's northernmost main island. For generations, fishermen there have flocked to the Ishikari River, where the salmon return to spawn every fall. For generations, too, they've enjoyed the area's namesake hot pot, cooked with their fresh catch. We got this authentic recipe from a restaurant owner whose great-grandfather opened the place in Ishikari Port in the nineteenth century to feed the crews of the local fishing boats. Along with salmon, this classic version of the dish calls for potatoes and yellow onions, vegetables introduced to Japan by Dutch traders about 400 years ago. You can cook the salmon with the skin on or off, as you desire. We prefer wild Alaskan king, sockeye, or Copper River salmon for this hot pot, but arctic char, sea trout, salmon trout, or farmed salmon work well, too.

SERVES 4

4 cups dashi (page 30)

$3/4$ cup shiro miso (page 15)

$1/4$ cup mirin

1 medium Spanish onion (about $3/4$ pound), cut crosswise into $1/2$-inch-thick slices

$1/4$ small head green cabbage (about $1/2$ pound), cut into bite-size pieces

2 medium Idaho potatoes (about 1 pound), peeled, halved lengthwise, and cut into $1/4$-inch-thick slices

$1/2$ package (about $1/2$ pound) firm tofu, cut into 4 pieces

1 ounce harusame (page 14), soaked in water for 15 minutes

1 negi (page 10), sliced on an angle into 2-inch pieces

$3^1/2$ ounces (half of a 200-gram package) enoki mushrooms, trimmed and pulled apart

4 ounces shiitake mushrooms (about 8 pieces), stemmed

1 pound salmon fillet, halved lengthwise and sliced into $1/2$-inch-thick pieces

2 cups shungiku leaves (page 11), stemmed

1 tablespoon salmon roe, for garnish (optional)

Sansho (page 18), for accent

Prepare the broth by combining the dashi, miso, and mirin in a bowl, whisking to blend well; reserve.

Place the onion slices on the bottom of a hot pot and randomly pile the cabbage and potatoes on top of it. Pour in the reserved broth. Cover the pot and bring it to a boil over high heat. Decrease the heat to medium and simmer for 3 minutes.

Uncover the pot, and place the tofu, *harusame*, *negi*, enoki mushrooms, and shiitake mushrooms on top of the other ingredients, arranging each in a separate, neat bunch. Cover the pot again and simmer for 5 minutes more.

Uncover the pot and arrange the salmon slices on top of the other ingredients. Simmer until the salmon

continued

is cooked through, about 5 minutes more. As the fish cooks, use chopsticks at regular intervals to separate the slices and press them into the broth so they heat through evenly. Add the *shungiku* leaves and simmer for 1 minute more. Garnish with a sprinkle of salmon roe, if using, over the pot.

Transfer the hot pot to the dining table. Serve the ingredients together with the broth in small bowls, accenting with the *sansho*.

Suggested side dish: *Individual bowls of steamed rice.*

VARIATIONS: While the recipe above is the Ishikari Port favorite, in other parts of Hokkaido, people like to add *sakekasu*, the deeply flavored lees of sake, milk, or even butter, a testament to the island's many dairy farms. (Lees, the residual rice mash from sake brewing, is difficult to find here but is sometimes sold frozen at Japanese markets.) Any of these will give the dish another wonderful layer of flavor. Add 2 tablespoons of *sakekasu* with the miso when mixing the broth, or 2 tablespoons butter or $1/2$ cup whole milk to the hot pot when adding the tofu and other ingredients.

MONKFISH HOT POT
Ankō Nabe

The most we usually see of monkfish—an ugly beast with a ferocious, tooth-filled jaw—is its flavorful loin, which resembles a lobster tail in appearance and texture. But not in Japan. There, families eat the entire fish, save that jaw, including the bones, skin, stomach, intestines, gills, and fins. And then there's the liver, as prized, tender, and sublime as foie gras. All of these parts go into a traditional monkfish hot pot, the liver caramelized together with miso to thicken and infuse the broth. In this recipe, we call just for the juicy loin, and if you can find it, that heavenly liver. Ask your local fish market if they can order one for you, it will be worth it. (Livers of monkfish caught in America, incidentally, are often shipped to Japan.) If you can't get monkfish liver, use the miso on its own, as we describe in the beginning of the recipe.

SERVES 4

$1/2$ **pound monkfish liver, cut into** $3/4$**-inch slices (optional)**

$1/2$ **cup aka miso (page 18)**

2 tablespoons mirin

4 cups dashi (page 30), or water, if using the liver

2 (6-inch) pieces kombu (only if using water)

1 ounce harusame (page 14), soaked in water for 15 minutes

$1/2$ **pound napa cabbage, sliced (page 52)**

$1/2$ **package (about** $1/2$ **pound) firm tofu, cut into 4 pieces**

$3^1/2$ **ounces (half of a 200-gram package) enoki mushrooms, trimmed and pulled apart**

6 ounces oyster mushrooms, trimmed and pulled apart

1 pound monkfish loin fillet, cut into $3/4$**-inch slices**

1 negi (page 10), sliced on an angle into 2-inch pieces

2 cups shungiku leaves (page 11), stemmed

$1/4$ **cup momiji oroshi (page 35), for garnish**

$1/2$ **cup shibori scallions (page 43), for garnish**

If using the optional monkfish liver:

Preheat a dry hot pot over medium heat. Add one-fourth of the monkfish liver and stir constantly for 1 minute to caramelize, mashing the liver as you stir. Add the miso, cooking and stirring for 1 minute more. Add the mirin, stir for 15 seconds, then add the 4 cups of water.

Place the kombu on the bottom of the hot pot. Add the *harusame*, cabbage, tofu, enoki mushrooms, and oyster mushrooms to the pot on top of the kombu, arranging each ingredient in a separate, neat bunch.

If using only miso:

Preheat a dry hot pot over medium heat. Add the miso, stirring and cooking for 1 minute to toast it. Add the mirin, stir for 15 seconds more, then add the dashi.

Add the *harusame*, cabbage, tofu, enoki mushrooms, and oyster mushrooms to the pot, arranging each ingredient in a separate, neat bunch.

For both:

Cover the hot pot and bring it to a boil over high heat. Decrease the heat to medium and simmer for 5 minutes. Uncover the pot and add the monkfish and *negi* (and the monkfish liver, if using), arranging them beside the other ingredients. Simmer until the fish is cooked through, about 10 minutes. Add the *shungiku* leaves and cook for 2 minutes more.

Transfer the hot pot to the dining table. Serve the ingredients together with the broth in small bowls. Garnish with the *momiji oroshi* and the *shibori* scallions.

Suggested shime: *Rice* ojiya *(page 24)*.

HALIBUT HOT POT
Inspired by Ara Nabe

Ara is a delicacy of the southern city of Fukuoka, a town with lively hot pot culture (see pages 95 and 130). A type of grouper that can grow five feet long, it hides in the reeds of a nearby bay, a wily creature that's a challenge to reel in. Restaurants in the area specialize in just this expensive fish. When we dropped into one of these places, we were treated to a leisurely hot pot procession that started with *ara* and *negi* served in fragrant broth, continued with *ara* shabu-shabu (see "Shabu-Shabu," page 63), followed with more *ara* in broth, this time with vegetables and tofu, before finishing with both rice *ojiya* and rice *zosui*. A whole lot of hot pot! While we dined on this firm, white-fleshed fish, we realized this dish would also work beautifully with fish we could find back home, like Alaskan halibut. Before cooking, lightly salt the fish to gently cure it. This concentrates its flavor and makes the flesh denser so it doesn't break apart simmering in the hot pot.

SERVES 4

1 pound halibut fillet

¹/₄ teaspoon salt, plus more for curing the fish

2 (6-inch) pieces kombu

1 ounce harusame (page 14), soaked in water for 15 minutes

¹/₂ pound napa cabbage, sliced (page 52)

1 negi (page 10), sliced on an angle into 2-inch pieces

¹/₂ package (about ¹/₂ pound) firm tofu, cut into 4 pieces

6 ounces oyster mushrooms, trimmed and pulled apart

3¹/₂ ounces (half of a 200-gram package) enoki mushrooms, trimmed and pulled apart

4 cups water

1 cup sake

1 cup ponzu (page 34), for dipping

¹/₄ cup momiji oroshi (page 35), for garnish

¹/₂ cup thinly sliced fresh chives, for garnish

To cure the halibut, very lightly salt it on both sides and place it in the refrigerator, loosely covered, for 30 minutes. Remove the fish, wipe off excess moisture on its surface with a paper towel, and cut into ¹/₂-inch-thick slices. Set aside.

Place the kombu on the bottom of a hot pot and the *harusame* over the kombu. Place the cabbage, *negi*, tofu, oyster mushrooms, and enoki mushrooms on top of the *harusame*, arranging each ingredient in a separate, neat bunch. Pour in the 4 cups water and the sake, and sprinkle in the ¹/₄ teaspoon salt.

Cover the hot pot and bring it to a boil over high heat. Decrease the heat to medium and simmer for 5 minutes. Uncover the pot and arrange the halibut slices on top of the other ingredients. Simmer until the fish is cooked through, about 5 minutes more.

continued

While the hot pot is simmering, pour the ponzu into four small bowls.

Transfer the hot pot to the dining table. Garnish the ponzu with the *momiji oroshi* and the chives. Dip the ingredients into the ponzu, and eat.

Suggested shime: *Rice* zosui *(page 24).*

VARIATIONS: You can also prepare this hot pot with cod, Chilean sea bass, turbot, pollack, North American grouper, or barramundi.

TABLESIDE COOKING OPTION: Arrange the ingredients on serving platters. After curing the halibut, do all the cooking at the dining table. Add the supporting ingredients all at once, or reserve half or more to cook later. Cook a little of the fish at a time.

SEA BASS SHABU-SHABU
Inspired by Tai Shabu-Shabu

Tai, or sea bream, has long been considered the "king of fish" in Japan. More than just a food, it's symbolic of happy occasions and traditionally served at birthdays, weddings, and other celebrations. Its tender, white flesh also makes it a classic ingredient for fast-cooking shabu-shabu, one of Japan's iconic hot pots. With shabu-shabu, you rapidly poach paper-thin slices of the fish in a simmering water-based broth, and eat in rounds. So you want to cook this dish on a portable burner set up on the dining table. (Before you do, please read "Shabu-Shabu," opposite.) In this recipe, we substitute sea bass for *tai*, which has a similar flavor and consistency, and is widely available here. We suggest you cut the fish into paper-thin slices, but thicker slices work nicely, too. Just cook them a little longer, until they're no longer translucent. You can enjoy this light, delicate hot pot throughout the year.

SERVES 4

- 1 pound sea bass fillet (striped bass or black sea bass), cut into $1/8$-inch-thick slices
- 4 ounces mizuna, trimmed and stems cut into 2-inch pieces
- $1/2$ package (about $1/2$ pound) firm tofu, cut into 4 pieces
- 1 negi (page 10), sliced on an angle into 2-inch pieces
- $3^1/2$ ounces (100-gram package) shimeji mushrooms, trimmed and pulled apart
- 7 ounces (200-gram package) enoki mushrooms, trimmed and pulled apart

- 1 napa cabbage–spinach roll, sliced (page 33)
- 1 cup ponzu (page 34), for dipping
- $1/4$ cup momiji oroshi (page 35), for garnish
- $1/2$ cup shibori scallions (page 43), for garnish
- 2 (6-inch) pieces kombu
- 1 ounce harusame (page 14), soaked in water for 15 minutes
- 5 cups water, plus more as needed
- 1 cup sake

Arrange the sea bass slices with the mizuna on a serving platter. Arrange the tofu, *negi*, *shimeji* mushrooms, enoki mushrooms, and slices of napa cabbage–spinach roll on other serving platters. Pour the ponzu into four small bowls, and place the *momiji oroshi* and *shibori* scallion garnishes in individual bowls.

Set up a portable burner on the dining table, and place a hot pot on top of it. Array the serving platters and the bowls with garnishes around the burner. Place a bowl of ponzu before each diner.

Place the kombu on the bottom of the hot pot and the *harusame* over the kombu. Add the tofu, *negi*, *shimeji* mushrooms, enoki mushrooms, and napa cabbage–spinach roll slices on top of the *harusame*, arranging each ingredient in a separate, neat bunch. (You can add all of the ingredients at once, or reserve half or more to cook later.) Pour in the 5 cups of water and the sake.

Cover the hot pot and bring it to a boil over high heat. Decrease the heat to medium and simmer for 5 minutes. Uncover the pot, and decrease the heat further to low.

Add some of the fish slices, arranging them in a single layer over the other ingredients. Poach until they're just cooked through, 15 to 30 seconds. To eat, garnish the ponzu with the *momiji oroshi* and the *shibori* scallions, and dip the fish into the ponzu.

Eat in rounds. Poach more fish in the gently simmering broth. Add some mizuna, and cook for 1 minute. Sample the other ingredients, also dipping them in the ponzu. If you reserved some of the tofu and vegetables, add them to the hot pot and cook, as you desire. Add more water to the pot, as needed.

Suggested shime: *Rice* zosui *(page 24).*

VARIATIONS: Shabu-shabu is also terrific with yellowtail, tuna, fluke, pink snapper, red snapper, sea trout (weakfish), squid, scallops, or octopus. Use the same quantity as in the recipe, cut into thin slices. You can also mix and match these ingredients to serve a fun "mixed seafood" shabu-shabu.

Shabu-Shabu

Shabu-shabu is the most refined expression of hot pot cooking. Paper-thin slices of seafood, beef, pork, or lamb are quickly poached in a water-based broth, then lightly dipped in a flavorful sauce. Like sashimi, it's an eating style that celebrates the Japanese devotion to *nama* (rawness)—the idea of experiencing pristine food as close to its natural state as possible. Like sashimi, too, it's subtle dining: the delicate broth and complementing dipping sauce never overwhelm the sublime intrinsic flavor of the main ingredients.

This is a dish you have to prepare at the dining table so as to enjoy the seafood or meat the instant they're ready. Simmer a broth-filled hot pot on a portable burner set up on the dining table, with the platters of food arrayed around it. The etiquette of shabu-shabu calls for the meal's host to add the foundation ingredients to the pot (vegetables and tofu), while individual diners cook their own slices of seafood or meat. To do so, grasp the slices with chopsticks and dunk them into the pot, sweeping them back and forth in the bubbling broth ("shabu-shabu" is said to be the sound an ingredient murmurs as it ripples through the liquid). As soon as the slices are blanched, they're ready; make sure not to overcook. Eat in leisurely, relaxed rounds, repeating with more slices, and sampling the other ingredients as soon as they cook through.

Use only sushi-grade seafood and the best cuts of meat for shabu-shabu. Try this enjoyable, social dish with fish (opposite), beef (page 117), pork (page 126), and lamb (page 134).

WHOLE FISH HOT POT
Sugata Nabe

This might be the easiest hot pot in the book to cook. It's certainly one of the easiest to like. Whole fish imbues the broth with tremendous flavor, especially from the bones and head. And the flesh comes out perfectly succulent, with the sake here removing fishiness, as it does in other seafood hot pots (see "The End of Fishiness," page 73). Poaching fish in this simple broth, then dipping into a light, citrusy ponzu, is a uniquely Japanese way of cooking, one that preserves the delicate taste of the fish and then enhances it with a light, umami-rich accent. Using the freshest, best-quality seafood is key for this dish. And don't miss out on the *shime*; the amazing, fish-infused rice *zosui* here is one of our favorites.

SERVES 4

1 whole red snapper (1½ to 2 pounds), cleaned and scaled (make sure the gills are removed)

Salt, for curing the fish

2 (6-inch) pieces kombu

½ pound napa cabbage, sliced (page 52)

4 cups water

1 negi (page 10), white part only, cut into 1-inch-long cylinders

7 ounces (two 100-gram packages) shimeji mushrooms, trimmed and pulled apart

1 cup sake

4 ounces mizuna, trimmed and stems cut into 2-inch pieces

1 cup ponzu (page 34), for dipping

¼ cup momiji oroshi (page 35), for garnish

½ cup shibori scallions (page 43), for garnish

Cut a large ½-inch-deep X into the flesh of the fish on both sides to help it absorb flavor when it cooks. To cure the fish, which allows its flavor to become more concentrated, lightly salt it on both sides and let it rest for 30 minutes at room temperature. Wipe off any excess moisture that appears on the fish's surface with a paper towel. Set aside.

Place the kombu on the bottom of a hot pot and pile the cabbage on top of it. Add the water, cover, and bring to a boil over high heat. Decrease the heat to medium, uncover the pot, and carefully place the fish inside. Place the *negi* and *shimeji* mushrooms around the sides of the fish. Pour in the sake. Cover and gently simmer on low

heat for 15 minutes. Uncover the pot, add the mizuna, and simmer for 1 minute more.

While the hot pot is simmering, divide the ponzu among four small bowls.

Transfer the hot pot to the dining table. Garnish the ponzu with the *momiji oroshi* and the *shibori* scallions. Dip the ingredients into the ponzu, and eat.

Suggested shime: *Rice* zosui *(page 24).*

VARIATIONS: You can also cook this hot pot with pink snapper, black sea bass, sea bream, dorade, or branzini.

YELLOWTAIL AND DAIKON HOT POT

Buri Daikon Nabe

Pairing yellowtail with daikon is a classic wintertime eating combination in Japan, as both ingredients taste best during the colder months. Yellowtail is caught wild all over Japan, and is also farmed. (The wild variety is typically called *buri*, the cultivated kind, *hamachi*.) It's a bold-flavored, steaklike fish, so it needs a strong soy sauce–laced broth like this one to stand up to it. The daikon helps to cut the yellowtail's fattiness and also soaks up delicious flavor as it cooks. Tadashi ate this hot pot every winter growing up—about as comforting as it gets!

SERVES 4

1 pound daikon, peeled, halved lengthwise, and cut into ¹/₂-inch-thick slices

2 cups dashi (page 30)

2 cups water

²/₃ cup mirin

²/₃ cup soy sauce

¹/₂ pound napa cabbage, sliced (page 52)

¹/₂ package (about ¹/₂ pound) firm tofu, cut into 8 slices

1 negi (page 10), sliced on an angle into 2-inch pieces

4 ounces shiitake mushrooms (about 8 pieces), stemmed and caps halved

1 pound yellowtail fillet, cut into 1-inch-thick slices

2 cups shungiku leaves (page 11), stemmed

Sansho (page 18), for accent

Add the daikon to a small saucepan and cover with water. Bring to a boil over high heat. Decrease the heat to medium and cook the daikon until it's tender, about 15 minutes. (Test by inserting a chopstick through the daikon. When the chopstick goes in easily, it's done.) Transfer the daikon to a colander and cool under running water; reserve.

Prepare the broth by combining the dashi, water, mirin, and soy sauce in a bowl; set aside.

Place the cabbage on the bottom of a hot pot. Add the tofu, daikon, *negi*, and shiitake mushrooms on top of the cabbage, arranging each ingredient in a separate, neat bunch. Pour in the reserved broth.

Cover the hot pot and bring it to a boil over high heat. Uncover the pot, and place the yellowtail on top of the other ingredients. When the broth returns to a boil, decrease the heat to medium. Simmer until the fish is cooked through, about 15 minutes. Add the *shungiku* leaves and cook for 2 minutes more.

Transfer the hot pot to the dining table. Serve the ingredients together with the broth in small bowls, accenting with the *sansho*.

Suggested shime: *Udon (page 26).*

VARIATIONS: You can also cook this hot pot with swordfish, mahi mahi, mako shark, Spanish mackerel, mackerel, sardines, or pompano.

BLACK COD AND SOY MILK HOT POT

Tōnyū Nabe

This is a warm and comforting winter favorite whose white broth turns Tadashi poetic—he says it reminds him of an icy lake. Black cod, also called sablefish, thrives in the frigid waters off Alaska and north of Hokkaido, Japan's northernmost island. As a result, the fish has a very high fat content, giving it silky textured, white flesh. This buttery richness serves as a nice complement to the natural sweetness of the soy milk in the dish. A word about soy milk: Avoid most supermarket varieties, which contain salt and other flavorings (even those marked "unsweetened") and are too watery. Purchase instead the soy milk sold at Japanese and Asian markets. This thicker, creamier liquid is made from just two ingredients—soybeans and water—and holds a lot more of that wonderful soybean flavor.

SERVES 4

1 pound black cod fillet

1/2 teaspoon salt, plus more for curing the fish

4 cups soy milk

1 cup dashi (page 30)

1/4 cup shiro miso (page 15)

1/2 pound napa cabbage, sliced (page 52)

1 negi (page 10), sliced on an angle into 2-inch pieces

1/2 package (about 1/2 pound) firm tofu, cut into 4 pieces

3 1/2 ounces (half of a 200-gram package) enoki mushrooms, trimmed and pulled apart

3 1/2 ounces (100-gram package) shimeji mushrooms, trimmed and pulled apart

4 ounces mizuna, trimmed and stems cut into 2-inch pieces

4 teaspoons wasabi, for accent

To cure the black cod so its flavor becomes more concentrated, lightly salt the fish on both sides and place in the refrigerator, loosely covered, for 1 hour. Remove the fish, wipe off excess moisture on its surface with a paper towel, and slice it into 3/4-inch pieces. Set aside.

Prepare the broth by combining the soy milk, dashi, the 1/2 teaspoon salt, and *shiro* miso in a bowl, whisking to blend well; reserve.

Add the cabbage, *negi*, tofu, enoki mushrooms, and *shimeji* mushrooms to a hot pot, arranging each ingredient in a separate, neat bunch. Pour in the broth.

Cover the hot pot and bring it to a boil over high heat. Decrease the heat to medium and simmer for 5 minutes. Uncover the pot and arrange the black cod slices on top of the other ingredients. Simmer until the fish is cooked through, 3 to 5 minutes. Add the mizuna and simmer for 1 minute more.

Transfer the hot pot to the dining table. Serve the ingredients together with the broth in small bowls, accenting with the wasabi.

Suggested shime: *Somen (page 26).*

KYOTO MACKEREL-MISO HOT POT
Saba Miso Nabe

For a country whose diet centers on fresh seafood, Kyoto, Japan's ancient capital, once faced a challenge: surrounded by mountains, in the old days it was a two-day walk from the ocean. A nearby bay teemed with mackerel, however, so fishermen there caught and salted the fish, and porters transported them to Kyoto by foot over the *saba kaido*—the mackerel road. Over time, this fish became the iconic seafood of the landlocked city. Salting not only cures the mackerel but mellows its strong oily flavor, too, which is further tempered in this traditional hot pot by blanching, and then pairing with sweet *saikyo* miso, another classic Kyoto ingredient. Make sure to carefully cook the delicate fish on a low simmer so it doesn't break apart. Mackerel, by the way, goes by a number of names, including Atlantic, Pacific, Boston, and Blue. Any of these varieties of mackerel work great for this dish.

SERVES 4

2 mackerel fillets (about 1 pound)

Salt, for curing the fish

1/4 pound daikon, peeled, quartered lengthwise, and cut into 1/4-inch-thick slices

2 cups dashi (page 30)

2 cups water, plus more for cooking

1/2 cup sake

1/2 cup saikyo miso (page 18)

1 tablespoon shiro miso (page 15)

1/2 pound napa cabbage, sliced (page 52)

1/2 package (about 1/2 pound) firm tofu, cut into 4 pieces

1 negi (page 10), white part only, cut on an angle into 2-inch pieces

4 ounces oyster mushrooms, trimmed and pulled apart

1/2 pound spinach, stemmed

4 teaspoons grated fresh ginger, for garnish

1/2 cup shibori scallions (page 43), for garnish

To cure the mackerel so its flavor becomes more concentrated, lightly salt the fish on both sides and place in the refrigerator, loosely covered, for 30 minutes.

Add the daikon to a small saucepan and cover with water. Bring to a boil over high heat. Decrease the heat to medium and cook the daikon until it's tender, about 5 minutes. Transfer the daikon to a colander and cool under running water. Set aside.

While the fish is curing, fill a saucepan with water and bring it to a boil over high heat, then decrease the heat to medium so the water simmers. Fill a large bowl with

water and set aside. When the mackerel is ready, slice it into 1-inch-thick pieces. Dip the slices into the simmering water for 15 seconds to quickly blanch them, then transfer the mackerel to the water-filled bowl. Once cooled, remove the fish, pat dry, and set aside.

Prepare the broth by combining the dashi, the 2 cups water, the sake, *saikyo* miso, and *shiro* miso in a bowl, whisking to blend well; reserve.

Place the cabbage on the bottom of a hot pot. Add the tofu, daikon, *negi*, and oyster mushrooms on top of the

continued

cabbage, arranging each ingredient in a separate, neat bunch. Pour in the reserved broth.

Cover the hot pot and bring it to a boil over high heat. Uncover the pot, decrease the heat to low, and add the mackerel in a separate pile. Gently simmer for 10 minutes. Add the spinach and simmer for 1 minute more.

Transfer the hot pot to the dining table. Serve the ingredients together with the broth in small bowls. Garnish with the grated ginger and *shibori* scallions.

Suggested shime: *Udon (page 26).*

The Power of Fish Bones

A few words about one of our favorite ingredients—fish bones. Humble fish bones (and heads and fins, too, if you can get your hands on them) beget fish stock, which imparts incredible *koku*—sublime depth of flavor—to hot pots, especially to the salmon, halibut, monkfish, and mackerel recipes in this chapter. We love cooking with fish stock, given that making it is a snap: First, place 1 pound of bones (and head and fins) in a large bowl and pour boiling water over them to cover. Mix once and strain, discarding the water (this removes blood and coagulated proteins, which can cloud the stock's flavor). Combine the bones (and head and fins) with 2 quarts of water and two 6-inch-long pieces of kombu in a stockpot. Bring to a boil, then simmer on low heat for 30 minutes. Check regularly to remove any scum that appears on the surface. Strain out the bones, and the stock is ready. If you can find fish bones at your local market, please give this stock a try; it'll add an amazing dimension to your dishes. Substitute the stock for the dashi in the salmon and mackerel recipes, for the water in the halibut recipe, and for the water or dashi in the monkfish recipe. Make sure to cook with the same bones and fish (for example, salmon bones for a salmon hot pot). This technique also works great with the fish mentioned in the recipe variations.

OLD TOKYO TUNA-BELLY HOT POT
Negima Nabe

Rich, buttery tuna belly might be the most coveted sushi bar selection the world over, but it wasn't always so prized. Hundreds of years ago, Tokyo Bay fishermen sold it off cheap because it spoiled quickly, and tuna's pink and ruby flesh reminded people of meat, prohibited by Buddhism at the time. Pushcart vendors, though, eventually hawked tuna belly simmered in soup, which evolved into this homey, traditional hot pot. Interestingly, despite its current popularity as sushi, as recently as Tadashi's childhood, tuna belly was always cooked, as it was considered too fatty to eat raw. This is a classic Tokyo dish, the savory-and-sweet broth exemplifying the bold tastes that define this city's cooking, with flavors hearty enough to stand up to this fish. The black pepper cuts the tuna belly's fattiness, but you can also achieve this effect with wasabi, *karashi* mustard, or *yuzu kosho*, if you prefer. You can substitute tuna belly with *chu toro* (the cut between tuna and tuna belly) or sushi-grade tuna. Just prepare either of these cuts rare; they dry out if overcooked.

SERVES 4

4 cups dashi (page 30)

³/₄ cup mirin

³/₄ cup soy sauce

1 package (7 ounces) itokonnyaku (page 14), well rinsed, strained, and quartered

3 negi (page 10), sliced on an angle into 2-inch pieces

¹/₂ pound napa cabbage, sliced (page 52)

¹/₂ package (about 6 ounces) broiled tofu, cut into 4 pieces

1 pound tuna belly (toro), cut into 1-inch cubes

Coarsely ground black pepper, for accent

Prepare the broth by combining the dashi, mirin, and soy sauce in a bowl; reserve.

Place the *itokonnyaku* noodles on the bottom of a hot pot. Add the *negi*, cabbage, and tofu on top of the *itokonnyaku*, arranging each ingredient in a separate, neat bunch. Pour in the reserved broth.

Cover the hot pot and bring it to a boil over high heat. Decrease the heat to medium, uncover the pot, and arrange the tuna belly beside the other ingredients. Simmer until the tuna belly is cooked rare to medium rare, 2 to 3 minutes.

Transfer the hot pot to the dining table. Serve the ingredients together with the broth in small bowls, accenting with the black pepper.

Suggested shime: *Soba (page 26).*

TABLESIDE COOKING OPTION: Arrange the ingredients on serving platters. After preparing the broth, do all the cooking at the dining table. Add the supporting ingredients all at once, or reserve half or more to cook later. Cook a little of the tuna belly at a time.

SARDINE DUMPLINGS HOT POT
Tsumire Nabe

This rustic hot pot is a fisherman family favorite. Sardines are plentiful and cheap, and you can eat all of the fish. In fact, if you were to visit a Japanese fishing port and watch a family make these dumplings, you'd notice the cooks there don't even bother gutting the fish—they just scale them and chop them, head, bones, and all. We use only the fillets for our dumplings, but if an occasional bone or two shows up, don't worry, they soften when they cook. Also, you don't have to shape these dumplings too perfectly; this is country cooking, after all. Besides good eating, the dumplings infuse the broth with incredible flavor, balanced nicely by the sake. If you'd like, you can add a dab of hot *karashi* mustard as an accent.

SERVES 4

SARDINE DUMPLINGS

12 sardines (about 2 pounds total), cleaned and filleted (ask your fish market to do this for you)

1/2 teaspoon salt

2 tablespoons cornstarch

2 teaspoons sake

1 teaspoon grated fresh ginger

1 large egg

1/2 cup scallions, coarsely chopped

—

1/2 cup soy sauce

1 cup sake

2 tablespoons mirin

4 cups water

2 (6-inch) pieces kombu

1/2 package (about 1/2 pound) firm tofu, shredded by hand into bite-size pieces

1/2 pound napa cabbage, sliced (page 52)

1 negi (page 10), sliced on an angle into 2-inch pieces

1/2 pound spinach, stemmed

To make the sardine dumplings, place the sardines, salt, cornstarch, sake, ginger, egg, and scallions in the work bowl of a food processor fitted with the metal blade. Pulse just until the mixture combines into a coarse paste. Transfer to a bowl and form into about a 1-inch-thick patty, which will make scooping simpler and faster. Set aside.

Prepare the broth by combining the soy sauce, sake, mirin, and water in a bowl. Set aside.

Add the kombu and the reserved broth to a hot pot and place over medium heat. As the broth is heating, scoop out teaspoonfuls of the sardine paste and add the paste to the hot pot, a teaspoon at a time. (Dip the spoon into the broth at regular intervals to make scooping easier.) Repeat until you've used all the sardine mixture. Once the dumplings have been formed, randomly pile the tofu, cabbage, and *negi* over them.

Cover the hot pot and bring it to a boil over high heat. Decrease the heat to medium, uncover the pot, and simmer for 5 minutes. Add the spinach and simmer for 1 minute more.

Transfer the hot pot to the dining table. Serve the ingredients together with the broth.

Suggested shime: *Somen (page 26).*

The End of Fishiness

If you want to eat fish but sometimes find it overpowering, the hot pots in this section offer a bit of piscine salvation. Because Japanese cuisine emphasizes a balance of flavors, traditional techniques have evolved to diminish the occasionally pronounced sense of "fishiness" in fish. The natural chemical compounds and flavors of miso and soy sauce temper bold fish like salmon, mackerel, monkfish, and yellowtail. Sake, added in these recipes to halibut, red snapper, sardines, and whole fish, works its own kind of alchemy: As its alcohol evaporates, fishiness vanishes with it, an effect affirmed by modern science. Salt curing, which we often call for as well, also has a palliative effect on fishiness. Finally, poaching in a hot pot—as opposed to sautéing, grilling, or frying—further mellows fish and infuses it with the flavors of the broth and other foods, making the succulent flesh even more delicious.

HIROSHIMA OYSTER HOT POT

Kaki Nabe

For a country renowned for its raw fish, oysters, surprisingly, are typically eaten cooked in Japan. The thinking is that cooking best brings out their briny, distinctive flavors, which you can't taste if you slurp them down raw and cold. Preparing oysters in hot pot is an old custom in Hiroshima, an area with a history of cultivating these mollusks that dates back hundreds of years, as well as an equally long tradition of producing miso. Marrying oysters and miso, two strong-tasting foods, as they do in Hiroshima, creates a very appealing balance of flavors. We blend three different misos to add a bit more complexity, but you can use one savory variety, if you'd like. Also, choose smaller Pacific oysters like Kumamoto or Hama Hama for this hot pot; the Pacific varieties, on the whole, are denser and less watery than their Atlantic cousins.

SERVES 4

1/3 cup Hatcho miso (page 18)

1/4 cup aka miso (page 18)

2 tablespoons saikyo miso (page 18)

1 cup sake

4 cups dashi (page 30)

1/2 pound napa cabbage, sliced (page 52)

1 ounce harusame (page 14), soaked in water for 15 minutes

1/2 package (about 1/2 pound) firm tofu, cut into 8 pieces

3 1/2 ounces (100-gram package) shimeji mushrooms, trimmed and pulled apart

1 negi (page 10), sliced on an angle into 2-inch pieces

2 dozen large raw oysters, shucked, cleaned, and shells discarded

2 cups shungiku leaves (page 11), stemmed

Sansho (page 18), for accent

Prepare the broth by combining the *Hatcho* miso, *aka* miso, *saikyo* miso, sake, and dashi in a bowl, whisking to blend well; reserve.

Place the cabbage on the bottom of a hot pot. Add the *harusame*, tofu, *shimeji* mushrooms, and *negi* on top of the cabbage, arranging each ingredient in a separate, neat bunch. Pour in the reserved broth.

Cover the hot pot and bring it to a boil over high heat. Decrease the heat to medium and simmer for 5 minutes. Uncover the pot, add the oysters in the center and the *shungiku* leaves in a pile next to them. When the liquid returns to a boil, simmer until the oysters cook through, 3 to 5 minutes.

Transfer the hot pot to the dining table. Serve the ingredients together with the broth in small bowls, accenting with the *sansho*.

Suggested shime: *Udon (page 26).*

VARIATION: If you own a Japanese hot pot—you need its lip and curved walls for this variation—you can prepare this dish in the most traditional way, called *dote*

continued

nabe. "*Dote*" refers to a riverbank, which is an apt image: Instead of adding the miso to the broth, mix the three misos together separately and set aside. After you pour the broth into the hot pot, spoon the miso mixture along the top inside edge of the hot pot, to create about a 1-inch-thick "bank" (the miso will stick to the lip). As you cook the hot pot, the miso will become toasted and dissolve in the broth, adding a lovely layer of caramelized flavor.

"SLEET" HOT POT

Mizore Nabe

This is another oyster hot pot, a specialty of the Miyagi Prefecture in the far north. The oysters there are often harvested wild, and are larger than the ones cultivated in Hiroshima. So use large Pacific oysters like Pacific Giant or Olympic Miyagi for this rustic dish. Unlike the Hiroshima version, we don't cook this hot pot with miso. Instead, we use sake and refreshing daikon to match the oysters' strong briny taste. The daikon here is grated, and when it's cooked in the hot pot, it resembles what weather forecasters like to euphemistically call a "wintry mix," thus, its name.

SERVES 4

1 pound daikon, peeled

4 cups dashi (page 30)

1 tablespoon usukuchi soy sauce (page 14)

1/4 cup sake

1 teaspoon salt

1 ounce harusame (page 14), soaked in water for 15 minutes

1/2 package (about 1/2 pound) firm tofu, cut into 8 pieces

1/2 pound napa cabbage, sliced into 1-inch squares

4 ounces oyster mushrooms, trimmed and pulled apart

1 negi (page 10), sliced on an angle into 2-inch pieces

2 dozen large oysters, shucked, cleaned, and shells discarded

4 teaspoons red yuzu kosho (page 20), for accent

Grate the daikon with the coarsest side of a box grater. Strain the grated daikon in a colander, discarding the liquid. Squeeze the daikon to remove any remaining liquid. Set aside.

Prepare the broth by combining the dashi, *usukuchi* soy sauce, sake, and salt in a bowl. Set aside.

Place the *harusame* on the bottom of a hot pot. Pile the tofu over it, then the cabbage and oyster mushrooms. Pour in the reserved broth.

Cover the hot pot and bring it to a boil over high heat. Decrease the heat to medium and simmer for 5 minutes.

Uncover the pot, drop the *negi* and oysters on top of the other ingredients, then add the grated daikon in a clump in the center. Cover the pot, increase the heat to high, and bring to a boil again. Uncover the pot, decrease the heat to low, and simmer until the oysters are cooked through, about 5 minutes.

Transfer the hot pot to the dining table. Serve the ingredients together with the broth in small bowls. Accent with the *yuzu kosho*.

Suggested shime: Inaniwa *udon (page 26).*

"SNOW" HOT POT
Yuki Nabe

This hot pot was inspired by a traditional *nagaimo*-infused soup. *Nagaimo* is a baton-shaped tuber with gooey, white-colored flesh, unlike any ingredient we typically encounter in America. (*Nagaimo* is a type of *yamaimo*, Japanese mountain yam, and is sometimes called that in stores.) Despite its unfamiliar slippery texture, it has a wonderful, clean taste. This tuber has long played an important role in Japanese cooking, like in this dish, where the *nagaimo* helps to highlight the natural sweetness of the scallops. When it's poured over the hot pot broth and cooked, it resembles snow—hence, the name—adding a delightful aesthetic touch. *Mitsuba* is an aromatic Japanese herb that provides a refreshing, green note, much like parsley does in Western cooking. Use both the leaves and the stems, as the stems hold a lot of flavor.

SERVES 4

1 pound nagaimo, peeled and coarsely chopped

4 cups dashi (page 30)

¼ cup mirin

1 tablespoon usukuchi soy sauce (page 14)

1 teaspoon salt

½ pound napa cabbage, sliced (page 52)

1 pound sea scallops

4 ounces shiitake mushrooms (about 8 pieces), stemmed

7 ounces (200-gram package) enoki mushrooms, trimmed and pulled apart

1 ounce harusame (page 14), soaked in water for 15 minutes

1 negi (page 10), sliced on an angle into 2-inch pieces

1 package mitsuba (about 1 ounce), leaves plucked and stems cut into 1-inch pieces, for garnish

Add the *nagaimo* to the jar of a blender, and pulse until it liquefies and becomes foamy. Do this in batches, if necessary. Set aside.

Prepare the broth by combining the dashi, mirin, soy sauce, and salt in a bowl. Set aside.

Place the napa cabbage on the bottom of a hot pot. Add the scallops, shiitake mushrooms, enoki mushrooms, *harusame*, and *negi* on top of the cabbage, arranging each ingredient in a separate, neat bunch. Pour in the reserved broth.

Cover the hot pot and bring it to a boil over high heat. Decrease the heat to medium and simmer for 5 minutes. Uncover the pot and pour in the *nagaimo*, spreading it on top of the other ingredients with chopsticks. Simmer for 3 minutes more.

Transfer the hot pot to the dining table. Serve the ingredients together with the broth in small bowls. Garnish with the *mitsuba*.

Suggested shime: *Rice* ojiya *(page 24).*

"STRAWBERRY" HOT POT
Ichigo Nabe

Like the "Snow" Hot Pot (page 78), this dish was also originally a traditional soup, in this case from old Tokyo, and dates back centuries to when the city was called Edo. The bright, pink-colored shrimp dumplings symbolize their namesake, strawberries, while spinach represents the berry's green leaves and stems, and shiitake mushrooms, the earth. Besides the imaginative presentation, these terrific dumplings have a pleasing springy texture and beautifully absorb all the flavors of the broth. If you can't find *nagaimo* (page 78), substitute 1 tablespoon cornstarch and 1 additional tablespoon of sake (for a total of 2 tablespoons of sake for the dumplings).

SERVES 4

SHRIMP DUMPLINGS

1 pound uncooked large shrimp, shelled, deveined, and coarsely chopped

1 teaspoon grated fresh ginger

1 tablespoon sake

1/4 teaspoon salt

2 tablespoons grated nagaimo (page 78), about 1 ounce nagaimo, peeled

—

4 cups dashi (page 30)

1/4 cup usukuchi soy sauce (page 14)

1/2 cup mirin

1/2 teaspoon salt

1/2 pound napa cabbage, sliced (page 52)

1 ounce harusame (page 14), soaked in water for 15 minutes

4 ounces shiitake mushrooms (about 8 pieces), stemmed

1/2 pound spinach, stemmed

Shichimi togarashi (page 18), for accent

To make the shrimp dumplings, place the shrimp, ginger, sake, salt, and *nagaimo* in the work bowl of a food processor fitted with the metal blade. Pulse just until they combine into a coarse paste. Transfer to a bowl and spread into a 1-inch-thick patty, which will make scooping simpler and faster. Set aside.

Prepare the broth by combining the dashi, soy sauce, mirin, and salt in a bowl; reserve.

Place the cabbage on the bottom of a hot pot, and add the *harusame* and shiitake mushrooms on top of it in separate, neat bunches. Pour in the reserved broth and place the pot over medium heat. As the broth is heating, scoop out teaspoonfuls of the shrimp paste and add the paste to the hot pot, a teaspoon at a time. (Dip the spoon into the broth at regular intervals to make scooping easier.) Repeat until you've used all the shrimp mixture. Simmer until the shrimp dumplings float to the surface, about 5 minutes.

Add the spinach alongside the other ingredients. Cover the pot and simmer for 2 minutes more.

Transfer the hot pot to the dining table. Serve the ingredients together with the broth in small bowls, accenting with the *shichimi togarashi*.

Suggested shime: *Rice* zosui *(page 24).*

SQUID HOT POT

Ishiri Nabe

This hot pot originated in the Noto Peninsula, a narrow strip of land that juts out like a finger into the Sea of Japan. The rural area is home to a morning market that has been going strong since the Middle Ages. Originating there as well is *ishiri*, a sauce made from fermented squid that dates back even farther than the market. Kin to the fish sauces of Southeast Asia, *ishiri* is pungent and salty, and adds a nice kick to dishes, much like nam pla does in Thai cooking. Here it naturally complements the hot pot's fresh squid. To finish tender, squid has to be cooked either very fast (under 2 minutes) or for at least 30 minutes—cooked anywhere in between, it will taste rubbery. We opt for the longer cooking time to give the squid a chance to leisurely absorb the broth's flavors. If you can't find *ishiri* sauce, substitute Thai nam pla or Vietnamese nuoc mam, both fermented fish sauces that offer a good approximation.

SERVES 4

4 cups water

1 cup sake

1/2 cup ishiri sauce

2 (6-inch) pieces kombu

1 pound squid, cleaned and cut into 1/2-inch rings (separate and use the tentacles)

1 ounce harusame (page 14), soaked in water for 15 minutes

1 napa cabbage–spinach roll, sliced (page 33)

1/2 package (about 1/2 pound) firm tofu, cut into 4 pieces

2 ounces daikon, peeled, quartered lengthwise, and cut into 1/4-inch-thick slices

1 negi (page 10), sliced on an angle into 2-inch pieces

4 ounces shiitake mushrooms (about 8 pieces), stemmed

3 1/2 ounces (100-gram package) shimeji mushrooms, trimmed and pulled apart

2 cups shungiku leaves (page 11), stemmed

1/4 cup momiji oroshi (page 35), for garnish

1/2 cup shibori scallions (page 43), for garnish

Prepare the broth by combining the water, sake, and *ishiri* sauce in a bowl; reserve.

Place the kombu on the bottom of a hot pot. Add the squid and the reserved broth. Cover and bring the hot pot to a boil over high heat. Decrease the heat to low and simmer until the squid becomes tender, about 30 minutes.

Uncover the pot and push the squid to one side. Add the *harusame*, slices of napa cabbage–spinach roll, tofu, daikon, *negi*, and the shiitake and *shimeji* mushrooms,

arranging each ingredient in a separate, neat bunch. Cover and simmer for 5 minutes. Uncover the pot again, add the *shungiku* leaves, and simmer for 1 minute more.

Transfer the hot pot to the dining table. Serve the ingredients together with the broth in small bowls. Garnish with the *momiji oroshi* and the *shibori* scallions.

Suggested shime: *Rice* ojiya *(page 24).*

FUKAGAWA CLAM HOT POT
Fukagawa Nabe

This is a hot pot for people in a hurry. It originated in Tokyo's old Fukagawa neighborhood, which sits by Tokyo Bay. For hundreds of years, busy craftsmen and fishermen made this place their home, and it once served as the city's central fish market. Two things have characterized the area's industrious citizens, and do to this day: They famously hate to wait. And they're known for their outsized generosity (a trait gleaned by living in densely packed wards—it helps to be neighborly). This hot pot, fast to prepare and easy to share, is a classic Fukagawa dish. It's traditionally cooked for just two people in a cast-iron pan (cast iron heats faster than clay). But why not slow down and make it for four, as in this recipe? At one time, Tokyo Bay was teeming with Asari clams, which made this dish an economical choice. If you can't find Asari, Manila or littleneck clams work fine, too.

SERVES 4

2 abura age cakes (page 14)

2 (6-inch) pieces kombu

2 negi (page 10), sliced thin on an angle

7 ounces (200-gram package) enoki mushrooms, trimmed and pulled apart

3/4 pound mizuna, trimmed and stems cut into 2-inch pieces

4 cups water, plus more for the abura age

1/2 cup plus 2 tablespoons shiro miso (page 15)

4 dozen clams, shucked, cleaned, and shells discarded

Shichimi togarashi (page 18), for accent

Fill a saucepan with water and bring it to a boil over high heat. Decrease the heat to medium and add the *abura age*. Boil for 1 minute to remove the excess oil from its surface. Strain the *abura age* and cut it into 1/2-inch-thick slices. Set aside.

Place the kombu on the bottom of a large skillet (a 12-inch cast-iron skillet is ideal). Place the reserved *abura age*, the *negi*, enoki mushrooms, and mizuna stems over the kombu, arranging each ingredient in a separate, neat bunch. Add the 4 cups water, then dab all the miso, a tablespoon at a time, over the other ingredients.

Place the skillet over high heat, and cook until the water boils. Decrease the heat to medium and simmer for 5 minutes, mixing the miso into the liquid at regular intervals with chopsticks. Add the mizuna leaves and the clams. Simmer until the clams are cooked through, 2 to 3 minutes.

Transfer the skillet to the dining table. Serve the ingredients together with the broth in small bowls, accenting with the *shichimi togarashi*.

Suggested shime: *Rice ojiya (page 24).*

TABLESIDE COOKING OPTION: Arrange the ingredients on serving platters. After preparing the *abura age*, do all the cooking at the dining table. Add the supporting ingredients all at once, or reserve half or more to cook later. Cook a little of the mizuna and clams at a time.

CRAB HOT POT
Kani Nabe

Crabs are plentiful in the Sea of Japan and crab hot pot is a gorgeous-looking dish that thrills families across the country. We're certain it will electrify your family and friends, too, but not only because it's so pretty: simmering the crab in the delicate, *usukuchi* soy sauce–infused broth magnifies its irresistible natural sweetness. We prefer Alaskan snow crab for this dish (snow crab is also caught off Japan's northern Hokkaido island), but King crab and Dungeness crab also work well. Eat the crab first, as soon as it's ready, followed by the other ingredients. That way, it will be at its most tender and will easily slide out of its shells. Japanese typically use a chopstick to pick crab meat from shells, but a crab fork is a practical option. Be sure to place a dish for the shells on the dining table.

SERVES 4

2 pounds crab, precooked or raw, cut into pieces

4 cups dashi (page 30)

$1/2$ cup usukuchi soy sauce (page 14)

$1/2$ cup mirin

1 ounce harusame (page 14), soaked in water for 15 minutes

1 napa cabbage–spinach roll, sliced (page 33)

$1/2$ package (about $1/2$ pound) firm tofu, cut into 4 pieces

1 negi (page 10), sliced on an angle into 2-inch pieces

$3^{1}/2$ ounces (100-gram package) shimeji mushrooms, trimmed and pulled apart

$1/4$ cup momiji oroshi (page 35), for garnish

$1/2$ cup shibori scallions (page 43), for garnish

To make the crab easier to eat, with a sharp, heavy knife, cut through the crab's leg joints, slice off strips of shell, and cut incisions into the claws.

Prepare the broth by combining the dashi, soy sauce, and mirin in a bowl. Set aside.

Place the *harusame* on the bottom of a hot pot. Add the crab, slices of napa cabbage–spinach roll, tofu, *negi*, and *shimeji* mushrooms over the *harusame*, arranging each ingredient in a separate, neat bunch. Pour in the reserved broth.

Cover the hot pot and bring it to a boil over high heat. Decrease the heat to medium and let simmer for 5 minutes more.

Transfer the hot pot to the dining table. Serve the ingredients together with the broth in small bowls. Garnish with the *momiji oroshi* and the *shibori* scallions.

Suggested shime: *Rice* zosui *(page 24).*

TABLESIDE COOKING OPTION: Arrange the ingredients on serving platters. After preparing the broth, do all the cooking at the dining table. Add the supporting ingredients all at once, or reserve half or more to cook later. Cook a little of the crab at a time.

PIRATE HOT POT
Kaizoku Nabe

This hot pot is attributed to Japanese pirates who once hid among the countless islands that dot the country's Inland Sea. We cook it with lobster and octopus, but you can add any other combination of seafood you'd like, including fish (white-fleshed types like red snapper), shrimp, or clams. Lobster has symbolic import in Japan, representing the elaborate helmets once worn by Japanese soldiers and seamen—a martial touch that explains, perhaps, why it's found in this pirate dish. After you boil it and cut it up, use the entire lobster in the hot pot, including the body, which imparts substantial character to the broth. Like squid, octopus has to be cooked either very fast or very slow to turn out tender, not rubbery. For this hot pot, long simmering is best.

SERVES 4

1 tablespoon salt

2 live lobsters (about 1½ pounds each)

2 cups dashi (page 30)

2 cups water, plus more for cooking the lobster

1 cup sake

½ cup mirin

½ cup usukuchi soy sauce (page 14)

½ pound precooked frozen octopus, thawed and cut into bite-size pieces

½ pound napa cabbage, sliced (page 52)

½ package (about ½ pound) firm tofu, cut into 4 pieces

1 ounce harusame (page 14), soaked in water for 15 minutes

1 negi (page 10), sliced on an angle into 2-inch pieces

3½ ounces (100-gram package) shimeji mushrooms, trimmed and pulled apart

2 cups shungiku leaves (page 11), stemmed

4 teaspoons red yuzu kosho (page 20), for accent

½ cup shibori scallions (page 43), for garnish

Fill a large stockpot with water and add the salt. Cover and bring to a boil over high heat. Uncover, add the lobsters, and boil them for 5 minutes. Drain, and cool the lobsters under running water. Cut the lobsters into pieces and crack their claws, to make them easier to eat. Set aside.

Prepare the broth by combining the dashi, the 2 cups water, sake, mirin, and soy sauce in a bowl; reserve.

Add the octopus and the reserved broth to a hot pot. Cover and bring the hot pot to a boil over high heat.

Decrease the heat to low and simmer until the octopus is tender, about 30 minutes.

Uncover the pot and add the cabbage, tofu, *harusame*, *negi*, *shimeji* mushrooms, and lobster. Cover and simmer for 5 minutes. Uncover the pot, add the *shungiku* leaves, and simmer for 1 minute more.

Transfer the hot pot to the dining table. Serve the ingredients together with the broth in small bowls. Accent with the red *yuzu kosho* and garnish with the *shibori* scallions.

Suggested shime: *Udon (page 26).*

BAY SCALLOPS AND SEA URCHIN HOT POT

Hokkai Nabe

Sapporo, the capital of the northern main island of Hokkaido, is truly fish heaven. When we visited that city's wholesale fish market at 4:30 one morning, the cavernous hall was filled with thousands of Styrofoam boxes coddling pristine cod, salmon, tuna, crab, and shrimp—more than 150 seafood varieties in all. We saw bay scallops in their shells and just-harvested sea urchin, and learned that they star in this local hot pot. Here at home, you can buy outstanding fresh bay scallops from Nantucket Bay and creamy sea urchin from California. If you have trouble finding sea urchin, substitute salmon roe, flying fish roe, smelt roe, or bottarga (Mediterranean cured roe).

SERVES 4

4 cups dashi (page 30)

1/2 cup mirin

1/2 cup usukuchi soy sauce (page 14)

1/2 pound napa cabbage, sliced (page 52)

1 ounce harusame (page 14), soaked in water for 15 minutes

1/2 package (about 1/2 pound) firm tofu, halved lengthwise and cut into 8 slices

3 1/2 ounces (100-gram package) shimeji mushrooms, trimmed and pulled apart

7 ounces (200-gram package) enoki mushrooms, trimmed, pulled apart, and halved

1 pound bay scallops

1 negi (page 10), cut into 1-inch-long cylinders

2 ounces fresh sea urchin (about 10 large pieces)

1 package mitsuba (about 1 ounce), page 78, leaves plucked and stems cut into 1-inch pieces

4 teaspoons wasabi, for accent

Prepare the broth by combining the dashi, mirin, and soy sauce in a bowl. Set aside.

Place the cabbage on the bottom of a hot pot and pile the *harusame* on top of it. Lay the tofu over the *harusame* and randomly cover with the *shimeji* mushrooms and enoki mushrooms. Pour in the reserved broth.

Cover the hot pot and bring it to a boil over high heat. Decrease the heat to medium and simmer for 5 minutes. Uncover the pot and add the scallops and *negi*. Simmer until the scallops are cooked through, about 5 minutes more. Check at regular intervals to skim any scum that appears on the surface. Gently lay the sea urchin pieces on top of the other ingredients. Sprinkle the *mitsuba*

on top. Cover and simmer until the sea urchin is heated through, about 30 seconds.

Transfer the hot pot to the dining table. Serve the ingredients together with the broth in small bowls, accenting with the wasabi.

Suggested shime: *Rice* ojiya *(page 24).*

TABLESIDE COOKING OPTION: Arrange the ingredients on serving platters. After preparing the broth, do all the cooking at the dining table. Add the supporting ingredients all at once, or reserve half or more to cook later. Cook a little bit of the scallops and sea urchin at a time.

"ANYTHING GOES" HOT POT
Yose Nabe

Seafood. And chicken. An unusual combination, perhaps, but "Anything Goes" won't go without them. This dish is considered the archetypical hot pot of Japan, refined and urbane—so it's got to look sharp. Keep aesthetics in mind when arranging the ingredients in the pot. A renowned Osaka City *yose nabe* restaurant inspired this particular recipe, the ingredients here attesting to the awesome diversity of foods available in that serious eating town, whether farmed, raised, or fished. They serve a practical purpose, too, melding together to add depth and fragrance to the dish. Use shrimp with their heads on, if you can find them, because the heads lace the broth with even more flavor. Feel free, too, to play around with the mix of seafood, or add more of one or less of another. The chicken, however, has to stay.

SERVES 4

4 cups dashi (page 30)

1/2 cup mirin

1/2 cup usukuchi soy sauce (page 14)

1 chicken leg and thigh (1/2 to 3/4 pound), boned, skinned, and cut into bite-size pieces

1/2 pound napa cabbage, sliced (page 52)

1 ounce harusame (page 14), soaked in water for 15 minutes

1 napa cabbage–spinach roll, sliced (page 33)

1/2 package (about 1/2 pound) firm tofu, cut into 4 pieces

4 littleneck clams

4 jumbo shrimp, fresh with head on, or frozen and thawed

4 large sea scallops

1/2 pound red snapper or sea bass fillet, cut into 1-inch slices

1 negi (page 10), sliced on an angle into 2-inch pieces

3 1/2 ounces (half of a 200-gram package) enoki mushrooms, trimmed and pulled apart

4 ounces oyster mushrooms, trimmed and pulled apart

1/2 medium carrot (about 2 ounces), peeled, cut into 2-inch pieces, then thinly sliced lengthwise

1/4 cup momiji oroshi (page 35), for garnish

1/2 cup shibori scallions (page 43), for garnish

Prepare the broth by combining the dashi, mirin, and soy sauce in a bowl. Set aside.

Fill a saucepan with water and bring it to a boil over high heat. Add the chicken and blanch for 1 minute. Strain the chicken in a colander and cool under running water.

Place the cabbage on the bottom of a hot pot. On top of the cabbage, add the *harusame*, slices of napa cabbage–spinach roll, tofu, clams, shrimp, scallops, red snapper, chicken, *negi*, enoki mushrooms, oyster mushrooms, and carrot, arranging each ingredient in a separate, neat bunch. Pour in the reserved broth.

continued

Cover the hot pot and bring it to a boil over high heat. Decrease the heat to medium, uncover the pot, and simmer for 10 minutes.

Transfer the hot pot to the dining table. Serve the hot pot ingredients and broth in small bowls. Garnish with *momiji oroshi* and the *shibori* scallions.

Suggested shime: *Udon (page 26).*

VARIATIONS: You can also cook this hot pot with lobster, razor clams, mussels, scallops, bay scallops, whiting, cod, halibut, or turbot.

TABLESIDE COOKING OPTION: Arrange the ingredients on serving platters. After preparing the broth and blanching the chicken, do all the cooking at the dining table. Add the supporting ingredients all at once, or reserve half or more to cook later. Cook a little of the seafood and chicken at a time.

Clockwise from top left: BUILDING A HOT POT

ODEN

A wintertime favorite, *oden* is dished up at restaurants, peddled from push carts, and is even found simmering at the local Japanese 7-Eleven. It's also a simple and popular hot pot to prepare at home. *Oden* varies widely by region, city, and often family, with some two dozen different ingredients added to this slow-cooking dish, depending on locale. But there are some mainstays: boiled eggs, daikon, *konnyaku*, fish cakes, and a dab of sharp *karashi* mustard. The recipe below is for the Tokyo-style *oden* that Tadashi grew up with. *Konnyaku* is a firm gelatin derived from a type of root, enjoyed for its chewy texture. *Ganmodoki* are fried tofu balls mixed with vegetables, while *iwashi tsumire*, *Satsuma age*, and *hanpen* are kinds of fish balls and fish cake. All are available at Japanese markets (also check the freezer section). The boiled eggs in this dish are amazing as they slowly absorb the tasty broth while they simmer, becoming dense and tinted with soy sauce. Finally, *oden* tastes just as good reheated the next day—the perfect leftovers.

SERVES 4

4 large eggs

8 ounces daikon, peeled and cut into $1/2$-inch-thick slices

$1/2$ package ($4^1/2$ ounces) konnyaku, cut into 4 wedges

4 pieces small ganmodoki

4 cups dashi (page 30)

$1/2$ cup mirin

$1/2$ cup soy sauce

2 (6-inch) pieces kombu

1 package (about 4 ounces) iwashi tsumire

1 package (about 3 ounces) Satsuma age

1 packages (about 4 ounces) hanpen, cut into 4 wedges

2 teaspoons karashi mustard (page 20), for accent

Place the eggs in a medium saucepan, cover with water, and bring to a boil over high heat. Boil, uncovered, for 5 minutes. Remove from the heat, drain, and peel the eggs under running water. The shelled eggs will feel soft to the touch. Set aside.

Cut a $1/8$-inch-deep X into the surface of one side of each daikon slice to help it absorb the aromatic cooking liquid. Place the daikon slices in a saucepan, cover with water, and bring to a boil over high heat. Decrease the heat to medium and simmer until the daikon is tender, about 10 minutes. (Test by inserting a chopstick through the daikon. When it goes in easily, it's done.) Strain the daikon and set aside.

Place the *konnyaku* in a saucepan, cover with water, and bring to a boil over high heat. As soon as the water reaches a boil, remove from the heat, strain the *konnyaku*, and set aside.

Place the *ganmodoki* in a colander set over a bowl or the sink and pour boiling water over it to wash off excess oil from its surface. Set aside.

Prepare the broth by combining the dashi, mirin, and soy sauce in a bowl; reserve.

continued

Place the kombu on the bottom of a hot pot. Place the eggs, daikon, *konnyaku*, *ganmodoki*, *iwashi tsumire*, and *Satsuma age* over the kombu, arranging each ingredient in a separate, neat bunch. Pour in the reserved broth.

Cover the hot pot and bring it to a boil over high heat. Decrease the heat to low and gently simmer for at least 1 hour (2 hours is ideal). Check the hot pot at regular intervals to make sure the ingredients are submerged in the broth. If the hot pot needs more liquid, add water.

Uncover the pot 5 minutes before serving, remove the kombu, and set aside to cool slightly. Lay the *hanpen* on top of the other ingredients. Cover the pot again and simmer for 5 minutes more.

As soon as the reserved kombu is cool enough to handle, cut it lengthwise into ½-inch-wide strips. Tie each strip into a bow. When the hot pot is finished cooking, add the kombu bows, arranging them in a separate, neat bunch.

Transfer the hot pot to the dining table. Serve the ingredients together with the broth in small bowls, accenting with the *karashi* mustard.

TABLESIDE COOKING OPTION: After removing the kombu and adding the *hanpen*, almost at the end, transfer the hot pot to the dining table. Finish cooking as described above. Oden is incredibly warm and comforting bubbling on a portable burner while you serve it.

CHICKEN AND DUCK

HAKATA CHICKEN HOT POT
Tori Mizutaki

The Kawasaki family of Hakata, a historic section of the southern city of Fukuoka, graciously shared this local recipe with us. In an area proud of its chicken—four heirloom varieties are raised in the nearby countryside—this hot pot is more than just a meal. As Mrs. Kawasaki explained, in Hakata, the dish is a tableside eating tradition that can last for up to four hours. The evening we visited, the family started the meal with bowls of *negi* and broth, followed by chicken and broth, then vegetables and broth. At that stage, Mrs. Kawasaki added chicken neck, liver, gizzard, and heart to the hot pot, before ending with rice *ojiya*. Wow. For a bit of variety, we suggest finishing the hot pot with somen, but if you prefer rice *ojiya*, we know Mrs. Kawasaki would be pleased. You can also enjoy this dish with ponzu on the side, dipping the ingredients into the citrusy sauce, a favorite way to enjoy it in the summer.

SERVES 4

4 chicken legs and thighs (2 to 3 pounds), skinned, boned, and cut into bite-size pieces

2 (6-inch) pieces kombu

¼ small head green cabbage (about ½ pound), cut into bite-size pieces

1 (7-ounce) package itokonnyaku (page 14), well rinsed, strained, and quartered

½ package (about ½ pound) firm tofu, cut into 4 pieces

1 negi (page 10), white part only, sliced on an angle into 2-inch pieces

4 ounces shiitake mushrooms (about 8 pieces), stemmed

3½ ounces (100-gram package) shimeji mushrooms, trimmed and pulled apart

½ medium carrot (about 2 ounces), peeled, cut into 2-inch pieces, and thinly sliced lengthwise

2 teaspoons salt

4 cups chicken stock (page 32)

2 cups shungiku leaves (page 11), stemmed

½ cup shibori scallions (page 43), for garnish

4 teaspoons green yuzu kosho (page 20), for accent

Fill a large stockpot with water and bring it to a boil over high heat. Add the chicken. When the water returns to a boil, poach for 1 minute. Remove from the heat, strain the chicken in a colander, and cool under running water. Set aside.

Place the kombu on the bottom of a hot pot and add the cabbage over it. Add the chicken, *itokonnyaku*, tofu, *negi*, shiitake and *shimeji* mushrooms, and carrot on top of the cabbage, arranging each ingredient in a separate, neat bunch. Sprinkle in the salt and add the chicken stock.

Cover the hot pot and bring it to a boil over high heat. Decrease the heat to medium and simmer for 10 minutes. Uncover the pot, add the *shungiku* leaves, and simmer for 1 minute more.

Transfer the hot pot to the dining table. Serve the ingredients together with the broth in small bowls. Garnish with the *shibori* scallions and accent with the green *yuzu kosho*.

Suggested shime: *Somen (page 26).*

continued

TABLESIDE COOKING OPTION: Arrange the ingredients on serving platters. After poaching the chicken, do all the cooking at the dining table. Add the supporting ingredients all at once, or reserve half or more to cook later. Cook a little bit of the chicken and *shungiku* at a time.

NAGOYA CHICKEN SUKIYAKI

Nagoya Tori Suki

Like the chickens raised in the Hakata area (Hakata Chicken Hot Pot, page 95), the heirloom breed of Nagoya City, in central Japan, is also a prized local ingredient. Theirs is called Nagoya Cochin, and is so pristine it's enjoyed as sashimi (yes, raw). In this local hot pot, the chicken is paired with dense, meaty, all-soybean *Hatcho* miso, the original version of which has been produced for over 600 years by two Nagoya-area companies. The sliced chicken breasts in the recipe readily absorb the beautiful *Hatcho* miso flavor, turning them incredibly juicy and tender. Use the best quality chicken you can buy. In Japan, this dish is typically prepared in a special cast-iron pan, but we use a cast-iron skillet instead. The cooked ingredients are dipped into beaten raw egg to add an appealing richness and silky texture, the traditional accent for sukiyaki. (You can skip this step, if you wish; this hot pot also tastes great without the egg.)

SERVES 4

- 2 cups sake
- 1/2 cup Hatcho miso (page 18)
- 2 tablespoons sugar
- 1 tablespoon vegetable oil
- 2 skinless, boneless chicken breasts (1 to 1 1/2 pounds), cut into 1/4-inch slices
- 1/2 pound napa cabbage, sliced (page 52)
- 1 negi (page 10), sliced on an angle into 2-inch pieces
- 1/2 medium Spanish onion (about 6 ounces), cut crosswise into 1/2-inch-thick slices
- 1/2 package (about 6 ounces) broiled tofu, cut into 4 pieces
- 6 ounces oyster mushrooms, trimmed and pulled apart
- 3 1/2 ounces (100-gram package) shimeji mushrooms, trimmed and pulled apart
- 2 cups shungiku leaves (page 11), stemmed
- 4 very fresh large eggs
- Sansho (page 18), for accent

Prepare a miso mixture by combining 1 cup of the sake, the *Hatcho* miso, and sugar in a bowl, whisking to blend well. Set aside.

Place a large skillet (a 12-inch cast-iron skillet is ideal) over medium heat. Add the oil. When the skillet is hot, add the chicken, stirring and cooking until the chicken turns golden, about 2 minutes.

Push the chicken to one side of the skillet, and add the cabbage, *negi*, onion, tofu, oyster mushrooms, and *shimeji* mushrooms, arranging each ingredient in a neat, separate bunch. Add the remaining 1 cup of the sake, and cook for 30 seconds. Pour in the reserved miso mixture.

Increase the heat to high to bring the liquid to a boil. Decrease the heat to medium and simmer for 10 minutes. Add the *shungiku* leaves and simmer for 1 minute more.

While the sukiyaki is simmering, crack 1 egg into each of four small bowls. Beat the eggs.

Transfer the skillet to the dining table. Dip the ingredients into the beaten egg, and eat. Accent each bowl with the *sansho*.

Suggested shime: Yaki udon *(page 27)*.

OLD TOKYO CHICKEN HOT POT
Mōryō Nabe

Mōryō is a mythical creature, bipedal and exceedingly hairy. So why name a hot pot after it? In this humble dish, chicken and kombu are first boiled, then finely shredded. Hundreds of years ago, in what is today Tokyo, it must have reminded some imaginative soul of the hirsute beast. The name stuck. Cooking earthy burdock together with chicken, like we do in this dish, is a classic pairing in Japanese cuisine; poaching teases out and mingles their tastes. This hot pot produces divinely moist and tender chicken, while the daikon and mizuna stems retain their pleasing character, a delightful contrast of textures. You can enjoy this dish all year around, and substitute ponzu for the *warijoyu*, if you desire. Also, instead of dipping the foods in the *warijoyu* or ponzu, you can eat them with the light broth, garnishing with grated fresh ginger and salt to taste.

SERVES 4

- 1/2 pound burdock root, cleaned (page 11)
- Distilled white vinegar or rice vinegar, for soaking burdock
- 2 (6-inch) pieces kombu
- 2 skinless, boneless chicken breasts (1 to 1 1/2 pounds)
- 5 cups water

- 1/2 pound daikon, peeled and cut into 1/8-inch-thick matchsticks (julienne)
- 4 ounces mizuna, trimmed and stems cut into 2-inch pieces
- 1/2 cup warijoyu (page 45), for dipping
- 1 tablespoon grated fresh ginger, for garnish
- 1/4 cup shibori scallions (page 43), for garnish

Cut the burdock like you are sharpening the point of a pencil to produce thin shavings. Place the shavings in a bowl of water treated with vinegar (1 teaspoon vinegar per cup of water), so the burdock doesn't oxidize and discolor. Set aside. (Strain before using.)

Place the kombu on the bottom of a hot pot and add the burdock and chicken breasts on top of it. Pour in the 5 cups water. Cover the pot and bring it to a boil over high heat. Decrease the heat to medium and uncover the pot. Skim off the scum on the surface with a kitchen spoon. Cover the pot again and simmer for 10 minutes.

Remove from the heat and uncover the pot. Transfer the chicken and kombu to a cutting board, reserving the broth in the pot. As soon as the chicken is cool enough to handle, shred it by hand into thin strips. Cut the kombu into strips about 1/8 inch thick and 2 inches long.

Randomly pile the chicken, kombu, daikon, and mizuna stems into the hot pot. Cover the pot and bring it to a boil over high heat. Decrease the heat to medium and simmer for 5 minutes. Uncover the pot, place the mizuna leaves on top of the other ingredients, and simmer for 1 minute more.

While the hot pot is simmering, pour the *warijoyu* into four small bowls, garnishing each with the grated ginger and the *shibori* scallions.

Transfer the hot pot to the dining table. Dip the ingredients in the *warijoyu*, and eat. Add more grated ginger and scallions, to taste.

Suggested shime: *Soba (page 26). Add the remaining* warijoyu *to the broth.*

AKITA HUNTER HOT POT
Kiritanpo Nabe

The Akita Prefecture in Japan's rugged far north is famous for its heavy snow, eponymous breed of dog, and *matagi*, legendary hunters who tramped through the mountains there in pursuit of bear, fox, deer, and other prey. These *matagi* carried with them *kiritanpo*, rice pounded into a cylindrical shape, then roasted. This dense, efficient nourishment traveled well and could be reheated in a hot pot bubbling over a campfire deep in the forest. Today, classic *kiritanpo* hot pot is prepared with burdock, *maitake* mushrooms (difficult to find here, so we use oyster mushrooms instead), and Hinai-jidori, a prized local breed of chicken, with the rice cylinders simmering in the deeply nuanced chicken-stock broth. You can make the *kiritanpo* up to a day ahead of time (up to broiling and cutting them in half). Refrigerate until you're ready to use them.

SERVES 4

2 cups hot cooked rice (page 36)

4 cups chicken stock (page 32)

1/4 cup mirin

1/2 cup soy sauce

2 (6-inch) pieces kombu

1 (7-ounce) package shirataki (page 14), well rinsed, strained, and quartered

1/4 pound burdock root, sliced and poached (page 49)

2 chicken legs and thighs (1 to 1 1/2 pounds), skinned, boned, and cut into bite-size pieces

1/2 pound napa cabbage, sliced (page 52)

1 negi (page 10), sliced on an angle into 2-inch pieces

3/4 pound oyster mushrooms, trimmed and pulled apart

2 cups shungiku leaves (page 11), stemmed

Shichimi togarashi (page 18), for accent

To make the *kiritanpo*, place the cooked rice in a bowl and mash the rice with the bottom of a ladle until the grains are crushed. Divide the mashed rice into 4 equal mounds. Wet your hands and scoop up a mound of the mashed rice. Wrap the rice around a wooden chopstick or thick bamboo skewer, forming it into a cylinder about 8 inches long and 1/2 inch thick. Make sure to pack the rice tight so it won't fall apart when cooking. Repeat with the remaining rice, yielding 4 *kiritanpo*, each on a chopstick. Wrap any exposed parts of the chopsticks in aluminum foil, to keep them from burning.

Preheat a broiler. When it's hot, broil the *kiritanpo* for about 2 minutes on each side, until they become lightly browned. Be careful not to burn them. Cool the *kiritanpo* to room temperature and slide them off the chopsticks. Halve each on an angle. Set aside.

Prepare the broth by combining the chicken stock, mirin, and soy sauce in a bowl. Set aside.

Place the kombu on the bottom of a hot pot and the *shirataki* over it. Add the burdock, chicken, cabbage, *negi*, and oyster mushrooms on top of the *shirataki*, arranging

continued

each ingredient in a separate, neat bunch. Pour in the reserved broth.

Cover the hot pot and bring it to a boil over high heat. Decrease the heat to medium and simmer for 10 minutes. Uncover the pot and add the reserved *kiritanpo* and the *shungiku* leaves, arranging these ingredients in separate, neat bunches. Simmer for 3 minutes more.

Transfer the hot pot to the dining table. Serve the ingredients together with the broth in small bowls, accenting with the *shichimi togarashi*.

CHICKEN AND MILK HOT POT
Asuka Nabe

Chicken and milk may seem like an unusual pairing, but think of this hot pot like a comforting French blanquette de veau and it starts to make a lot of sense. Instead of rich cream, though, this recipe calls for milk and chicken stock, which give it a much lighter touch. This dish is absolutely delicious, perfect for a frosty winter day, and a favorite with kids, too. When we've tried it out on family and friends, the verdict was always the same—they loved it. This hot pot is named after the period in ancient Japanese history that coincides with the arrival of Buddhism. At the time, meat and some milk was consumed in Japan, but shortly thereafter it was banned for a thousand years on religious grounds. Once the hot pot simmers for a while, you may notice the milk in the broth separating, but that's normal (from heating milk protein) and it won't affect the taste.

SERVES 4

2 (6-inch) pieces kombu

¼ small head green cabbage (about ½ pound), cut into bite-size pieces

1 ounce harusame (page 14), soaked in water for 15 minutes

½ package (about ½ pound) firm tofu, cut into 4 pieces

1 cup chicken stock (page 32)

¼ cup mirin

4 cups whole milk

2 teaspoons salt

4 chicken legs and thighs (2 to 3 pounds), boned, skinned, and cut into bite-size pieces

1 negi (page 10), sliced on an angle into 2-inch pieces

7 ounces (200-gram package) enoki mushrooms, trimmed and pulled apart

½ pound spinach, stemmed

4 teaspoons grated fresh ginger, for garnish

Place the kombu on the bottom of a hot pot and randomly pile the cabbage, *harusame*, and tofu over it. Add the chicken stock and mirin. Cover the hot pot and bring it to a boil over high heat. Uncover the pot and add the milk, salt, and chicken. Decrease the heat to medium and gently simmer for 10 minutes. Be careful the milk doesn't boil over.

Add the *negi* and enoki mushrooms and simmer for 3 minutes more. Add the spinach and simmer for 1 minute more, until it cooks through.

Transfer the hot pot to the dining table. Serve the ingredients together with the broth, garnishing with the grated ginger.

Suggested shime: *Mochi (page 27).*

SUMO WRESTLER HOT POT

Chanko Nabe

A gracious sumo wrestler taught us how to prepare this hot pot. Eighteen years old and north of 380 pounds, he was the *chanko cho* (chief hot pot cook) of his sumo stable, as the teams who live, eat, and train together are known. These wrestlers follow a fixed daily schedule: train hard in the morning, enjoy hearty *chanko* for lunch, and nap in the afternoon. But a hot pot every day? The sumo explained that there are numerous varieties of *chanko* (which means "father and child," symbolizing sumo togetherness). All are a snap to whip up, nutritious, and, most importantly, delicious, making it easy to down the massive quantities needed to gain sumo-level heft. This hot pot is one of his favorites, with mouthwatering chicken dumplings and fresh pork belly. Sumo-style hot pot, albeit in daintier quantities, is extremely popular throughout Japan. It's the perfect dish for the high school football (or basketball or hockey or . . .) star sitting at your own dinner table.

SERVES 4

CHICKEN DUMPLINGS

2 chicken legs and thighs (1 to 1½ pounds), boned, skinned, and coarsely chopped

1 teaspoon chopped fresh ginger

1 tablespoon aka miso (page 18)

1 large egg

¼ cup chopped scallions

—

4 cups chicken stock (page 32)

½ cup sake

2 teaspoons salt

½ small head green cabbage (about 1 pound), cut into bite-size pieces

2 cloves garlic, finely chopped

½ package (about ½ pound) firm tofu, cut into 4 pieces

1 negi (page 10), sliced on an angle into 2-inch pieces

1 medium Spanish onion (about ¾ pound), cut crosswise into ½-inch-thick slices

4 ounces shiitake mushrooms (about 8 pieces), stemmed

3½ ounces (half of a 200-gram package) enoki mushrooms, trimmed and pulled apart

½ pound fresh pork belly, thinly sliced ⅛ inch thick (ask your butcher, or see page 115) and slices halved

4 teaspoons green yuzu kosho (page 20), for accent

To make the chicken dumplings, place the chicken, ginger, miso, egg, and scallions in the work bowl of a food processor fitted with the metal blade. Pulse just until the mixture becomes a coarse paste. Transfer to a bowl and form into a 1-inch-thick patty, which will make scooping simpler and faster. Set aside.

Prepare the broth by combining the chicken stock, sake, and salt in a bowl; reserve.

Place the cabbage and garlic on the bottom of a hot pot. Pour in the broth. Cover the hot pot and bring it to a boil

continued

over high heat. Uncover the pot, and decrease the heat to medium so the liquid simmers.

Push the cabbage to one side of the hot pot. Scoop out teaspoonfuls of the chicken dumpling paste and add the paste to the hot pot, a teaspoon at a time. (Dip the spoon into the broth at regular intervals to make scooping easier.) Repeat until you've used all the chicken mixture. Simmer until the chicken dumplings float to the surface, about 3 minutes.

Add the tofu, *negi*, onion, shiitake mushrooms, and enoki mushrooms to the hot pot, arranging each ingredient in a separate, neat bunch. Cover and simmer for 5 minutes. Uncover the pot and lay the pork belly slices on top of the other ingredients. When the hot pot returns to a boil, simmer until the pork belly is cooked through, about 5 minutes more.

Transfer the hot pot to the dining table. Serve the ingredients together with the broth in small bowls, accenting with the *yuzu kosho*.

Suggested shime: *Ramen (page 26).*

TABLESIDE COOKING OPTION: Arrange the ingredients on serving platters. After preparing the chicken dumpling paste and broth, do all the cooking at the dining table. You can add the supporting ingredients all at once, or reserve half or more to cook later. Cook a little of the chicken dumplings and pork belly at a time.

CHICKEN CURRY HOT POT

Karé Nabe

Thank the Japanese navy for this dish; its sailors learned about Indian curry from British seamen they met back in the nineteenth century, and brought it home with them (India, of course, was still ruled by Britain then). Curry evolved into its own uniquely sweet-and-spicy version in Japan, and eventually became extremely popular across the country. It became a particular favorite with kids, as Tadashi can attest—when he was young, curry was his and his sisters' favorite treat. Curry also evolved into a beloved hot pot, enjoyed together by family and friends. While the spice comes in many blends, for this dish we prefer the standard curry powder sold at supermarkets, which adds a nice combination of fragrance, flavor, and a touch of heat. Also, while we suggest a bowl of steamed rice on the side for this dish, udon *shime* is outrageously good here, too.

SERVES 4

4 cups chicken stock (page 32)

$^1/_4$ cup sake

$^1/_3$ cup soy sauce

1 tablespoon sugar

1 tablespoon vegetable oil

2 boneless, skinless chicken breasts (1 to 1$^1/_2$ pounds), cut into $^1/_4$-inch-thick slices

1 medium Spanish onion (about $^3/_4$ pound), cut crosswise into $^1/_2$-inch-thick slices

$^1/_4$ cup curry powder

$^1/_4$ small head green cabbage (about $^1/_2$ pound), cut into bite-size pieces

2 stalks celery (about $^1/_4$ pound), sliced on an angle into 3-inch-long pieces, $^1/_4$ inch thick

1 medium carrot (about $^1/_4$ pound), peeled and sliced on an angle into 3-inch long pieces, $^1/_4$ inch thick

1 medium Idaho potato (about $^1/_2$ pound), peeled and cut into $^1/_4$-inch-thick slices

2 cloves garlic, chopped

1 teaspoon chopped fresh ginger

1 negi (page 10), sliced on an angle into 2-inch pieces

Prepare the broth by combining the chicken stock, sake, soy sauce, and sugar in a bowl. Set aside.

Add the oil to a hot pot and place over medium heat. When the oil is hot, add the chicken, stirring and cooking until the chicken turns golden, about 2 minutes. Add the onion, stirring and cooking for 2 minutes. Add the curry powder, stirring and cooking for 1 minute more to caramelize. Add the reserved broth.

Randomly pile the cabbage, celery, carrot, potato, garlic, and ginger into the pot. Cover and bring to a boil over high heat. Decrease the heat to medium and simmer for 10 minutes. Uncover the hot pot and add the *negi*. Simmer until the chicken is cooked through, about 5 minutes longer.

Transfer the hot pot to the dining table. Serve the ingredients together with the broth in small bowls.

Suggested side dish: *Individual bowls of steamed rice.*

DUCK AND DUCK DUMPLING HOT POT

Kamo Nabe

This rustic dish hails from the rugged Japanese Alps, where hunters have long bagged fowl like duck and pheasant. The duck is dusted in soba flour before being poached in a tasty broth. Why soba flour? The soba locks in the duck's natural juices as it cooks, absorbs the dish's many flavors, and naturally complements the distinctive taste of the bird. So each tender slice has a lot going on. And so does the broth, laced as it is with the essence of the duck dumplings and the earthy burdock. Be sure to try the *shime* here, too—the soba noodles are incredible. When making the dumplings, be careful not to pulse the mixture in the food processor for too long. If the paste becomes too smooth, the dumplings can turn hard when they cook.

SERVES 4

DUCK DUMPLINGS

1 boneless duck breast (about $1/2$ pound), skinned and coarsely chopped

2 tablespoons buckwheat flour

$1/4$ cup thinly sliced scallions

$1/2$ teaspoon sansho (page 18)

1 teaspoon sake

1 large egg

—

2 boneless duck breasts (about 1 pound), one skinless, one with skin

$1/4$ cup buckwheat flour

3 cups water

$1/2$ cup mirin

$3/4$ cup soy sauce

2 (6-inch) pieces kombu

2 negi (page 10), sliced on an angle into 2-inch pieces

$1/4$ pound burdock root, sliced and poached (page 49)

$1/2$ pound napa cabbage, sliced (page 52)

1 (7-ounce) package shirataki (page 14), well rinsed, strained, and quartered

$1/2$ package (about $1/2$ pound) firm tofu, cut into 4 pieces

$1/2$ pound spinach, stemmed

4 teaspoons wasabi, for accent

To prepare the duck dumplings, place the duck, buckwheat flour, scallions, *sansho*, sake, and egg in the work bowl of a food processor fitted with the metal blade. Pulse just until the mixture becomes a coarse paste. Transfer to a bowl and form into a 1-inch-thick patty, which will make scooping simpler and faster. Set aside.

Freeze the duck breasts for 20 minutes to make them easier to slice. While the duck is chilling, place the buckwheat flour in a bowl. Remove the duck breasts from the freezer and cut them into $1/4$-inch-thick slices. Dredge the duck slices, one at a time, in the buckwheat flour. Set aside.

Prepare the broth by combining the water, mirin, soy sauce, and kombu in a hot pot. Cover the pot and place it over high heat.

As soon as the liquid boils, uncover the pot and decrease the heat to medium. Scoop out teaspoonfuls of the duck dumpling paste and add the paste to the hot pot, a teaspoon at a time. (Dip the spoon into the broth at regular intervals to make scooping easier.) Repeat until you've used all the duck mixture. Simmer until the duck dumplings float to the surface, about 3 minutes. Once the duck dumplings are ready, add the *negi*, burdock, cabbage, *shirataki*, and tofu to the hot pot, arranging each ingredient in a separate, neat bunch. Cover the pot and simmer for 5 minutes.

Uncover the pot and add the duck slices in an overlapping row, as well as the spinach. Simmer for 3 to 5 minutes more, depending on if you like the duck cooked rare or medium.

Transfer the hot pot to the dining table. Serve the ingredients together with the broth in small bowls, accenting with the wasabi.

Suggested shime: *Soba (page 26).*

VARIATION: If you can find a whole duck at your butcher, or are a hunter who just bagged a plump mallard, try preparing the hot pot with the entire bird. This is the original, rustic version of the dish (the one at left is a simpler preparation). It requires more work, but yields more succulent dumplings and an even tastier broth. Here's what to do: Butcher a whole duck. Bone and skin the legs and thighs and use the meat to make the dumplings (the legs and thighs are a richer cut). Reserve the breasts to slice for the hot pot, as described in the recipe. Finally, use the carcass, leg bones, and wings to make a duck stock (following the chicken stock recipe, page 32, but with duck bones). Substitute this stock for the water in the recipe. If you're truly duck *otaku* (duck obsessed, in a good way), this variation will blow you away.

TABLESIDE COOKING OPTION: Arrange the ingredients on serving platters. After preparing the duck dumplings and duck breast slices, and adding the liquids to the hot pot, do all the cooking at the dining table. Add the supporting ingredients all at once, or reserve half or more to cook later. Cook the duck slices like shabu-shabu (see "Shabu-Shabu," page 63), a little bit at a time.

DUCK GYOZA HOT POT
Kamo Gyoza Nabe

Crescent-shaped dumplings wrapped in a flour skin, gyoza are originally an import from China. They're enormously popular in Japan, enjoyed both at restaurants and at home, and even deified at Gyoza Stadium, a "food theme park" in Osaka City. Gyoza hot pot is a family favorite, too, especially with kids. Relatives and friends often gather not only to eat them, but also to wrap the dumplings together ("the gyoza party"). While gyoza are typically prepared with pork, we think the duck in this recipe is particularly amazing. We suggest dipping the dumplings into a chili-infused sauce, but you can also enjoy them served just with the broth (add a little salt, to taste). Use the thickest wonton skins you can find for the dumplings, so they hold together as they cook. (Chinese wonton skins are typically thicker than their Japanese counterparts; both are usually sold frozen, in packages of about fifty skins.) Also, a rubber spatula is an indispensable tool for preparing the gyoza mixture.

SERVES 4

DUCK GYOZA

1 cup finely chopped green cabbage (about 4 ounces)

Salt

1 boneless duck breast with skin (about $1/2$ pound), coarsely chopped

3 tablespoons chopped scallions

$1/4$ teaspoon salt

1 teaspoon chopped fresh ginger

1 clove garlic, chopped

1 tablespoon sake

1 tablespoon shiro miso (page 15)

$1/4$ cup finely chopped garlic chives (nira, about 1 ounce)

1 package (about 50 skins) round wonton skins

1 teaspoon cornstarch mixed with $1/2$ cup warm water

DIPPING SAUCE

4 tablespoons soy sauce

2 tablespoons rice vinegar

1 tablespoon ra yu (Japanese chili oil, also called la yu)

2 tablespoons thinly sliced scallions

—

2 (6-inch) pieces kombu

$1/2$ pound napa cabbage, sliced (page 52)

1 ounce harusame (page 14), soaked in water for 15 minutes

5 cups chicken stock (page 32)

$1/2$ cup sake

1 teaspoon salt

1 negi (page 10), sliced on an angle into 2-inch pieces

4 ounces shiitake mushrooms (about 8 pieces), stems removed

$3^{1}/2$ ounces (half of a 200-gram package) enoki mushrooms, trimmed and pulled apart

$1/4$ pound spinach, stemmed

continued

To make the duck gyoza filling, in a bowl, lightly salt the chopped green cabbage, toss to mix well, and allow it to rest at room temperature for 15 minutes. In batches, place the cabbage on a clean kitchen towel and wring the towel over the sink to squeeze out excess moisture. Set aside.

Place the duck, scallions, salt, ginger, garlic, sake, and miso in the work bowl of a food processor fitted with the metal blade. Pulse just until the mixture becomes a coarse paste. Transfer to a bowl and fold in the reserved cabbage and the garlic chives, mixing well.

To assemble the gyoza, place a wonton skin in the palm of one hand. Spoon a teaspoon of the gyoza mixture onto the center of the wonton skin. With your finger, wet the wonton skin's edges with the cornstarch-water mixture. Fold the skin in half and pinch it together. (The cornstarch will "glue" the wonton skin together.) Place the gyoza on a plate and repeat with the rest of the mixture, which will make about 25 pieces. Be sure to keep the wonton skins covered with a moist paper towel while you work, so they don't dry out. Set the gyoza aside.

To make the dipping sauce, combine the soy sauce, rice vinegar, chili oil, and the scallions. Set aside.

Place the kombu on the bottom of a hot pot, and pile the napa cabbage and *harusame* on top of it. Add the chicken stock, sake, and salt, and bring to a boil over high heat. Remove the kombu and discard. Decrease the heat to medium and add the *negi*, shiitake mushrooms, and enoki mushrooms. Simmer for 2 minutes. Add the gyoza to the hot pot, making sure they're submerged in the broth. Simmer until the gyoza are cooked through, 5 to 10 minutes (check by opening one up at the 5-minute mark). Add the spinach and simmer for 1 minute more.

While the hot pot simmers, fill four small bowls with the dipping sauce.

Transfer the hot pot to the dining table. Dip the ingredients into the sauce-filled bowls, and eat. Add more dipping sauce to the bowls.

Suggested shime: *Rice* zosui *(page 24).*

TABLESIDE COOKING OPTION: Arrange the ingredients on serving platters. After preparing the gyoza and dipping sauce, do all the cooking at the dining table. Add the supporting ingredients all at once, or reserve half or more to cook later. Cook a few of the gyoza at a time.

"REFRIGERATOR" HOT POT

Here's a timesaver that Tadashi uses at home when it's dinner in a hurry: open the refrigerator, gather whatever fresh ingredients you have, drop them in a hot pot, and cook. Hot pots are a perfect way to mix and match typical refrigerator finds like broccoli, cauliflower, tomatoes, pork, chicken—anything you wish—with traditional foundation ingredients like napa cabbage, *negi*, and *harusame*. Two choices for broth: soy sauce–based, as used in "Anything Goes" Hot Pot, page 89, or miso-based, like in Hiroshima Oyster Hot Pot, page 75. So get creative—and invent your own hot pot.

BEEF, PORK, LAMB, AND VENISON

BEEF SUKIYAKI

Sukiyaki

A favorite celebration food in Japan, sukiyaki is enjoyed to mark a graduation, birthday, or promotion at the office. Sugar and beef give it its cachet. Back in the nineteenth century, they were both pricey and relatively rare. So much so, that in a testament to its value, the beef in this hot pot was typically seared in a cast-iron sukiyaki pan and eaten first, before the other ingredients. Some people still enjoy sukiyaki this way, but we cook it in a more contemporary style, with all the ingredients simmering in the pan together. Besides symbolizing luxury, sugar and beef have a practical side, too: the sugar and the caramelized beef produce a tasty flavor combination that infuses the vegetables and tofu in the dish. Like with Nagoya Chicken Sukiyaki (page 96), dip the cooked ingredients into raw egg to eat, a traditional accent that adds silky texture and balances the meatiness of the dish. (You can skip this step, if you wish; this hot pot tastes great without the egg, too.)

SERVES 4

- 1 tablespoon beef fat, trimmed from the beef (below)
- 1 pound strip loin or rib eye, thinly sliced 1/8 inch thick (ask your butcher, or see "How to Slice Meat for Hot Pot," opposite page)
- 1/2 medium Spanish onion (about 6 ounces), cut crosswise into 1/2-inch-thick slices
- 1/2 package (about 6 ounces) broiled tofu, cut into 4 pieces
- 1/2 pound napa cabbage, sliced (page 52)
- 1 negi (page 10), sliced on an angle into 2-inch pieces
- 4 ounces shiitake mushrooms (about 8 pieces), stems removed
- 7 ounces (200-gram package) enoki mushrooms, trimmed and pulled apart
- 1 (7-ounce) package itokonnyaku, (page 14), well rinsed, strained, and quartered
- 2 cups sake
- 1/3 cup sugar
- 1/2 cup soy sauce
- 2 cups shungiku leaves (page 11), stemmed
- 4 very fresh large eggs

Preheat a large skillet (a 12-inch cast-iron skillet is ideal) over medium heat. When the skillet is hot, add the beef fat. Cook for 1 minute, coating the entire surface of the skillet with the fat. Add the beef, stirring and cooking until it browns on both sides, about 1 minute. Make sure to separate the slices while you stir.

Push the beef to one side of the skillet and add the onion, tofu, cabbage, *negi*, shiitake mushrooms, enoki mushrooms, and *itokonnyaku* to the skillet, arranging each ingredient in a separate, neat bunch. Pour the sake into the skillet.

Increase the heat to high. As soon as the sake starts boiling, simmer for 30 seconds. Sprinkle in the sugar, and pour the soy sauce over the other ingredients in the skillet. Decrease the heat to medium and simmer until the vegetables have become tender, about 10 minutes. Add the *shungiku* leaves in a pile over the beef and simmer for 1 minute more.

While the skillet is simmering, crack 1 egg into each of four small bowls. Beat the eggs.

Transfer the skillet to the dining table. Dip the ingredients into the beaten egg, and eat.

Suggested shime: *Prepare 4 individual bowls of steamed rice. Simmer the remaining broth over medium heat. One at a time, add 4 large eggs to the skillet and poach them in the cooking broth. When they're ready, dish them over the rice and top with the remaining broth. This shime is amazing for breakfast the next day, too.*

HOW TO SLICE MEAT FOR HOT POT

Japanese food markets typically sell meat already thinly sliced and hot pot ready, or you can ask your butcher to do it for you. If you want to slice the beef, pork, lamb, or venison for the hot pot recipes yourself, here's what you do: Freeze the meat until it partially hardens, 2 to 3 hours depending on your individual freezer. Remove the meat and slice it thinly against the grain with the sharpest knife you own. This partial freezing will firm up the meat and make it easier to cut.

BEEF SHABU-SHABU
Gyu Shabu-Shabu

Adapted from the hot pot traditions of China, shabu-shabu is prepared with a variety of ingredients (see "Shabu-Shabu," page 63). But beef is the classic version. While we're accustomed to dense steaks that are often aged, Japanese typically enjoy their beef tender, well marbled, and thinly sliced, like in this extremely popular dish. Here paper-thin meat is quickly poached and downed rare or medium rare—you want to see pink in the flesh. Dipping it into the sesame sauce adds a beautiful contrasting richness. Japanese markets typically sell shabu-shabu–style beef already sliced paper thin, but if you can't find it or your butcher can't do this for you, just follow our slicing method (see "How to Slice Meat for Hot Pot," page 115), cutting the beef as thin as possible. Depending on the thickness, you may have to poach the meat a few seconds longer. Shabu-shabu is a hot pot you have to cook on a portable burner on the dining table to best savor the beef and other ingredients as soon as they're ready. Like other shabu-shabu dishes, too, you can enjoy this one year round.

SERVES 4

SESAME DIPPING SAUCE

1/2 cup toasted white sesame seed

1 cup dashi (page 30)

3 tablespoons soy sauce

2 tablespoons sugar

1 tablespoon sake

1 tablespoon rice vinegar

1/2 teaspoon freshly ground black pepper

—

1 pound strip loin or rib eye, sliced paper thin (1/16 inch thick; see headnote)

1/2 pound spinach, stemmed

1/2 package (about 1/2 pound) firm tofu, cut into 4 pieces

1/2 pound napa cabbage, sliced (page 52)

1 negi (page 10), sliced on an angle into 2-inch pieces

3 1/2 ounces (half of a 200-gram package) enoki mushrooms, trimmed and pulled apart

4 ounces shiitake mushrooms (about 8 pieces), stems removed

2 (6-inch) pieces kombu

1 ounce harusame (page 14), soaked in water for 15 minutes

8 cups water, plus more as needed

1 teaspoon salt

To make the sesame dipping sauce, combine the sesame seed, dashi, soy sauce, sugar, sake, rice vinegar, and black pepper in the jar of a blender. Pulse until well combined (if you notice a few whole sesame seeds at the end, that's OK). Fill four small bowls with the sauce. Set aside.

Arrange the beef slices and spinach on a serving platter. Arrange the tofu, cabbage, *negi*, enoki mushrooms, and shiitake mushrooms on other serving platters.

continued

Set up a portable burner on the dining table, and place a hot pot on top of it. Array the serving platters around the burner. Place the bowls with sesame sauce before each diner.

Place the kombu on the bottom of the hot pot and the *harusame* over the kombu. Add the tofu, cabbage, *negi*, enoki mushrooms, and shiitake mushrooms on top of the *harusame*, arranging each ingredient in a separate, neat bunch. (You can add all of the ingredients at once, or reserve half or more to cook later.) Pour in the 8 cups of water and sprinkle in the salt.

Cover the pot and bring it to a boil over high heat. Decrease the heat to medium and simmer for 5 minutes. Uncover the pot and add some of the meat slices, arranging them in a single layer over the other ingredients. Poach for 15 to 30 seconds, until they cook rare or medium rare. Dip the meat into the sesame sauce to eat.

Eat in rounds. Poach more beef in the simmering broth. Add some spinach, and cook for 1 minute. Sample the other ingredients, also dipping them into the sesame sauce. If you reserved some of the tofu and vegetables, add them to the hot pot and cook as you desire. Add more water to the pot, as needed.

Suggested shime: *Udon (page 26). Dip the udon into the sesame sauce.*

VARIATION: Another popular way to enjoy shabu-shabu is dipped in ponzu (page 34), which is lighter than the sesame sauce. Garnish with *momiji oroshi* (page 35) and *shibori* scallions (page 43).

SHABU-SUKI

Shabu-Suki

Many of the hot pots in this book claim long pedigrees. Shabu-suki is not one of them. Shabu-suki, in fact, was invented by Tadashi in his home kitchen, an experiment by a hot pot–loving chef to marry the best qualities of sukiyaki with those of shabu-shabu. His family and coauthor agree: his creation is a mouthwatering success! Shabu-suki employs a flavorful sukiyaki-like broth (but lighter) and meat cut to sukiyaki-like thickness. You poach the beef, however, shabu-shabu style, and dip it into a shabu-shabu sauce, this one prepared with tangy *umeboshi*, a type of Japanese apricot that's salt-pickled. Enjoy the other ingredients à la sukiyaki, eaten together with the complex, tasty broth. You have to try this dish. Make sure to cook this dish like shabu-shabu (see "Shabu-Shabu," page 63), tableside on a portable burner.

SERVES 4

UMEBOSHI DIPPING SAUCE

10 small umeboshi

Umeboshi pickling liquid (whatever is left in the jar, up to 1 tablespoon)

1 cup sake

1/4 cup mirin

1/2 cup water

2 teaspoons wasabi (optional)

—

4 cups dashi (page 30)

2 cups sake

1 cup soy sauce

1 pound strip loin or rib eye, sliced 1/8 inch thick (ask your butcher, or see "How to Slice Meat for Hot Pot," page 115)

2 cups shungiku leaves (page 11), stemmed

1/2 package (about 1/2 pound) firm tofu, cut into 4 pieces

1/2 pound napa cabbage, sliced (page 52)

1 negi (page 10), sliced on an angle into 2-inch pieces

7 ounces (200-gram package) enoki mushrooms, trimmed and pulled apart

4 ounces shiitake mushrooms (about 8 pieces), stems removed

1 (7-ounce) package itokonnyaku (page 14), well rinsed, strained, and quartered

To make the *umeboshi* dipping sauce, first remove the pits from the pickled *umeboshi*. Add the pitted *umeboshi*, the pickling liquid, sake, mirin, and water to a small saucepan, and place over low heat. Cook for 10 minutes, stirring constantly and mashing the *umeboshi* so they break apart. Remove from the heat and let the sauce cool to room temperature. Mix in the wasabi. Fill four small bowls with the sauce. Set aside.

Prepare the broth by mixing the dashi, sake, and soy sauce in a bowl. Set aside.

Arrange the beef and *shungiku* leaves on a serving platter. Arrange the tofu, cabbage, *negi*, enoki mushrooms, and shiitake mushrooms on other serving platters.

Set up a portable burner on the dining table, and place a hot pot on top of it. Array the serving platters around the burner. Place a bowl filled with the dipping sauce before each diner.

Place the *itokonnyaku* on the bottom of the hot pot. Add the tofu, cabbage, *negi*, enoki mushrooms, and shiitake mushrooms on top of the *itokonnyaku*, arranging each ingredient in a separate, neat bunch. (You can add all of the ingredients at once, or reserve half or more to cook later.) Pour in the broth.

Cover the hot pot and bring it to a boil over high heat. Decrease the heat to medium and simmer for 5 minutes. Uncover the pot and add some of the beef slices, arranging them in a single layer over the other ingredients. Poach until they're cooked rare to medium rare, 15 to 30 seconds. Dip the meat into the *umeboshi* dipping sauce to eat.

Eat in rounds. Poach more meat in the simmering broth. Add some *shungiku*, and cook for 1 minute. Sample the other ingredients by eating them with the broth in separate bowls. If you reserved some of the tofu and vegetables, add them to the hot pot and cook as you desire.

Suggested shime: *Udon (page 26).*

YOKOHAMA BEEF HOT POT
Yokohama Gyu Nabe

Yokohama is a major Japanese port city where a population of American and other Western traders settled in the nineteenth century. Their presence there led to an embrace of things Western in Japan, including eating beef, which was long taboo in the country. Japanese cooks paired meat with bold flavors like miso and burdock, which turn out to be a terrific match, a sentiment we know you'll share when you taste this hearty, satisfying hot pot. Unlike the other beef hot pots, here the meat is cubed sirloin, a testament, perhaps, to American-style steak? Also, like with sukiyaki (Beef Sukiyaki, page 114), dip the cooked beef into raw egg to eat. (You can skip this step, if you wish; this hot pot tastes great without the egg, too.) You can also accent this dish with coarsely ground black pepper, *sansho*, or *karashi* mustard.

SERVES 4

2 cups sake

¼ cup Hatcho miso (page 18)

¼ cup aka miso (page 18)

¼ cup sugar

¼ pound burdock root, cleaned (page 11)

Distilled white vinegar or rice vinegar, for soaking burdock

1 pound sirloin steak, cut into 1-inch cubes, plus a 1-inch cube of beef fat

½ medium Spanish onion (about 6 ounces), cut crosswise into ½-inch-thick slices

½ package (about 6 ounces) broiled tofu, cut into 4 pieces

4 ounces shiitake mushrooms (about 8 pieces), stems removed

1 napa cabbage–spinach roll, sliced (page 33)

1 negi (page 10), sliced on an angle into 2-inch pieces

2 cups shungiku leaves (page 11), stemmed

4 very fresh large eggs

Prepare a miso mixture by combining 1 cup of the sake, the *Hatcho* miso, *aka* miso, and sugar in a bowl, whisking to blend well. Set aside.

Cut the burdock like you are sharpening the point of a pencil to produce thin shavings. Place the shavings in a bowl of water treated with vinegar (1 teaspoon vinegar per 1 cup of water) so the burdock doesn't oxidize and discolor. Set aside. (Strain before using.)

Place a large skillet (a 12-inch cast-iron skillet is ideal) over medium heat. When the skillet becomes hot, add the reserved beef fat. Cook for 1 minute, coating the entire surface of the skillet with the fat. Add the steak, stirring and cooking to brown the meat, about 2 minutes. Add the burdock shavings, stirring and cooking until they soften, about 1 minute.

Push the steak and burdock to one side of the skillet and add the onion, tofu, shiitake mushrooms, slices of napa cabbage–spinach roll, and *negi*, arranging each

continued

ingredient in a separate, neat bunch. Pour in the remaining 1 cup of sake and cook for 30 seconds. Pour in the reserved miso mixture. Simmer until the vegetables cook through, about 10 minutes. Add the *shungiku* leaves and simmer for 1 minute more.

While the skillet is simmering, crack the eggs into four bowls. Beat the eggs.

Transfer the skillet to the dining table. Dip the beef into the raw eggs to eat. Serve the other ingredients together with the broth in separate small bowls.

Suggested shime: Yaki udon *(page 27).*

BEEF AND TARO ROOT HOT POT
Imoni

In this rustic dish from Japan's far north, beef is paired with taro and burdock, two roots with distinctive, earthy flavors. Here the beef simmers on its own first to create a pure flavor that's then burnished with the essence of the other ingredients. This classic Japanese cooking approach (like Japanese Chicken Stock, page 32) is the opposite of a typical Western beef stew, where all the ingredients braise together from the start. This hot pot also works great with chicken or just vegetables. For a chicken-only version, substitute sliced boneless, skinless leg and thigh for the meat (cooking for only 10 minutes instead of 30 minutes in the first step), and use chicken stock instead of water. For vegetables, omit cooking the beef and use dashi (page 30) or mushroom stock (page 47) instead of water.

SERVES 4

- 1/2 pound stew meat, cut into bite-size cubes
- 2 (6-inch) pieces kombu
- 4 cups water
- 1/2 cup sake
- 1/4 pound burdock root, cleaned (page 11)
- Distilled white vinegar or rice vinegar, for soaking burdock
- 1/2 package (about 4 1/2 ounces) konnyaku (page 14)
- 1 medium carrot (about 1/4 pound), peeled, halved lengthwise, and cut into 1/2-inch-thick slices

- 1/4 pound daikon, peeled, quartered lengthwise, and cut into 1/2-inch-thick slices
- 6 small taro roots (about 1 pound), peeled and quartered lengthwise (halve if more than 2 inches long)
- 1/2 cup aka miso (page 18)
- 1 negi (page 10), sliced on an angle into 2-inch pieces
- 3 1/2 ounces (100-gram package) shimeji mushrooms, trimmed and pulled apart
- Shichimi togarashi (page 18), for accent

Add the stew meat, kombu, water, and sake to a hot pot. Cover the pot and bring it to a boil over high heat. Decrease the heat to medium, uncover the hot pot, and

simmer for 30 minutes. Check the pot at regular intervals to remove any scum that appears on the surface.

Meanwhile, slice the burdock into 2-inch pieces by cutting on an angle and rolling the root a quarter turn after each slice. Place the burdock pieces in a bowl of water treated with vinegar (1 teaspoon vinegar per 1 cup of water), so the burdock doesn't oxidize and discolor. Set aside. (Strain before using.)

Cut the *konnyaku* coarsely by scooping pieces out of it with a teaspoon; reserve.

Once the beef has cooked for 30 minutes, add the burdock to the hot pot, and simmer for another 15 minutes. Keep checking the pot at regular intervals to remove any scum that appears on the surface.

After 45 minutes, randomly pile the carrot, daikon, taro, and *konnyaku* into the pot. Spoon the miso into the center of the hot pot, on top of the other ingredients (it will dissolve as it cooks). Cover the pot and bring it to a boil over high heat. Decrease the heat to medium and simmer for 15 minutes.

Uncover the pot again, add the *negi* and *shimeji* mushrooms, and simmer for 5 minutes more.

Transfer the hot pot to the dining table. Serve the ingredients together with the broth in small bowls, accenting with the *shichimi togarashi*.

Suggested shime: *Mochi (page 27).*

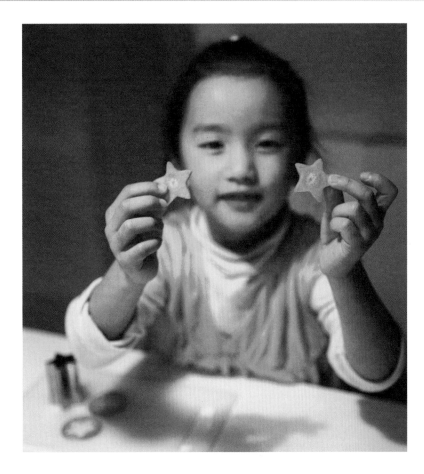

PORK SHABU-SHABU
Ton Shabu-Shabu

Bacon lovers young and old will relish this hot pot. The key to this particular shabu-shabu is the *negi*, whose acidity cuts the fattiness of the pork belly, a perfect balance of tastes. Just be careful not to overcook the *negi*, so it doesn't lose its crunch and bite. Also, to appreciate the full effect of this pairing, snare both ingredients with your chopsticks for each bite to savor together. This hot pot is light enough to serve all year around. Like with the other shabu-shabu dishes in the book, prepare this hot pot tableside on a portable burner (see "Shabu-Shabu," page 63).

SERVES 4

1 pound fresh pork belly, thinly sliced 1/8 inch thick (ask your butcher, or see "How to Slice Meat for Hot Pot," page 115) and halved

4 ounces mizuna, trimmed and stems cut into 2-inch pieces

1/2 pound napa cabbage, sliced (page 52)

1/2 package (about 1/2 pound) firm tofu, cut into 4 pieces

4 ounces shiitake mushrooms (about 8 pieces), stems removed

4 negi (page 10), white parts only, thinly sliced on an angle

1 cup ponzu (page 34), for dipping

4 teaspoons green yuzu kosho (page 20), for accent

2 (6-inch) pieces kombu

1 teaspoon salt

8 cups water, plus more as needed

Arrange the pork belly slices and mizuna on a serving platter. Arrange the cabbage, tofu, shiitake mushrooms, and *negi* on other serving platters. Pour the ponzu into four small bowls and add a dab of *yuzu kosho* to each.

Set up a portable burner on the dining table, and place a hot pot on top of it. Array the serving platters around the burner. Place a ponzu-filled bowl before each diner.

Place the kombu on the bottom of a hot pot and add the cabbage over it. Add the tofu and shiitake mushrooms on top of the cabbage, arranging the ingredients in separate, neat bunches. (You can add all of the ingredients at once, or reserve half or more to cook later.) Add the salt and the 8 cups water.

Cover the hot pot and bring it to a boil over high heat. Decrease the heat to medium and simmer for 5 minutes. Uncover the pot and sprinkle some *negi* on top of the other ingredients. Simmer for 1 minute. Add some of the pork slices, arranging them in a single layer over the other ingredients. Poach until they cook through, about 2 minutes. Eat the *negi* and pork together, dipping them into the ponzu.

Eat in rounds. Poach more *negi* and pork in the simmering broth. Add some mizuna, and cook for 1 minute. Sample the other ingredients, also dipping them into the ponzu. If you reserved some of the tofu and vegetables, add them to the hot pot and cook, as you desire. Add more water to the pot, as needed.

Suggested shime: *Somen (page 26).*

PORK MISO HOT POT

Buta Nabe

If you live somewhere cold, expedition-weight-long-johns cold, this comforting hot pot will warm your soul. In this dish, pork shoulder simmers in a hearty, miso-laced broth—irresistible savory flavors the whole family will enjoy. So simple and fast to prepare, this hot pot is a perfect candidate for regular dinner rotation. When we were discussing this recipe at Tadashi's house, his school-age daughters piped in with an enthusiastic two thumbs up. So you know it's got the kids' vote.

SERVES 4

4 cups water

1/2 cup aka miso (page 18)

2 (6-inch) pieces kombu

1/2 pound napa cabbage, sliced (page 52)

1 negi (page 10), sliced on an angle into 2-inch pieces

7 ounces (200-gram package) enoki mushrooms, trimmed and pulled apart

6 ounces oyster mushrooms, trimmed and pulled apart

1 (7-ounce) package shirataki (page 14), well rinsed, strained, and quartered

1/2 package (about 1/2 pound) firm tofu, cut into 4 pieces

1 pound boneless pork shoulder, sliced 1/8 inch thick (ask your butcher, or see "How to Slice Meat for Hot Pot," page 115)

Shichimi togarashi (page 18), for accent

Prepare the broth by combining the water with the miso, whisking to blend well; reserve.

Place the kombu on the bottom of a hot pot, and add the cabbage over it. Add the *negi*, enoki mushrooms, oyster mushrooms, *shirataki*, and tofu on top of the cabbage, arranging each ingredient in a separate, neat bunch. Pour in the reserved broth.

Cover the pot and bring to a boil over high heat. Uncover the pot and add the pork. Cover the pot again and bring to a boil over high heat once more. Decrease the heat to medium and simmer until the pork cooks through, about 5 minutes.

Transfer the hot pot to the dining table. Serve the ingredients together with the broth in small bowls. Accent with the *shichimi togarashi*.

Suggested shime: *Udon (page 26).*

PORK AND GREENS HOT POT
Wakakusa Nabe

Like Pork Shabu-Shabu (page 126), this simple, delectable hot pot can be enjoyed year round. Here the light broth is infused with pork belly and the saltier *usukuchi* soy sauce, which lavish the greens with mouthwatering, savory flavor. You can substitute one of the leaves with Shanghai bok choy or baby bok choy (make sure to chop the stems into small pieces, so they cook thoroughly). Or, you can double up on one type and use only two kinds of greens. As with everything else in hot pot cooking, it's up to your individual taste and preference.

SERVES 4

4 cups dashi (page 30)

1/2 cup mirin

1/2 cup usukuchi soy sauce (page 14)

1/2 pound napa cabbage, sliced (page 52)

1 negi (page 10), sliced on an angle into 2-inch pieces

1/2 pound fresh pork belly, thinly sliced 1/8 inch thick (ask your butcher, or see "How to Slice Meat for Hot Pot," page 115) and halved

1/2 pound spinach, stemmed

4 ounces mizuna, trimmed and stems cut into 2-inch pieces

2 cups shungiku leaves (page 11), stemmed

2 cups watercress (about 1/2 pound)

Ground white pepper, for accent

Prepare the broth by combining the dashi, mirin, and soy sauce in a bowl.

Add the napa cabbage and *negi* to a hot pot. Pour in the broth.

Cover the hot pot and bring it to a boil over high heat. Decrease the heat to medium, uncover the pot, and add the pork belly, arranging the slices on top of the other ingredients. When the hot pot returns to a boil, simmer for 3 minutes. Add the spinach, mizuna, *shungiku* leaves, and watercress in a random pile on top of the pork belly. Cover and simmer until the greens are cooked through, 2 to 3 minutes more.

Transfer the hot pot to the dining table. Serve the ingredients together with the broth in small bowls, accenting with the white pepper.

Suggested shime: *Udon (page 26).*

TABLESIDE COOKING OPTION: Arrange the ingredients on serving platters. After preparing the broth, do all the cooking at the dining table. Add the supporting ingredients all at once, or reserve half or more to cook later. Cook a little of the greens and pork belly at a time.

HAKATA PORK INTESTINES HOT POT

Motsu Nabe

A pair of friendly police officers invited us to share this hot pot with them in Hakata, a historic section of the southern city of Fukuoka. A ferry ride away from Korea, and as close to Shanghai as it is to Tokyo, Hakata has long been influenced by its Asian neighbors. You see this in the food, like with this Chinese-influenced dish, sumptuously flavored with chilies, garlic, and garlic chives. The officers told us that families in Hakata typically fall into two camps: pork-intestine-hot-pot-eating clans and Hakata-chicken-hot-pot-eating ones (page 95). But we're not taking sides—we love both. Some families add other organ meats like heart and stomach to pork intestine hot pots, which you can try, too. If you can't find fresh intestines, Chinese markets often sell them preboiled and frozen (so skip boiling in the first step).

SERVES 4

1 pound fresh pork intestines, washed well

4 cups chicken stock (page 32)

1 cup sake

1/4 cup mirin

3/4 cup soy sauce

5 Japanese chilies, soaked in hot water for 30 minutes and finely chopped

2 cloves garlic, chopped

1/2 small head green cabbage (about 1 pound), cut into bite-size pieces

1 negi (page 10), thinly sliced on an angle

4 ounces bean sprouts (about 2 cups)

4 ounces garlic chives (nira), cut into 3-inch pieces

If you're using fresh pork intestines, add them to a saucepan and cover with water. Bring to a boil over high heat. As soon as the water boils, strain the intestines and set aside.

Prepare the broth by combining the chicken stock, sake, mirin, and soy sauce in a bowl.

Add the pork intestines to a hot pot. Add the chilies and garlic, and pour in the broth. Pile the cabbage, *negi*, bean sprouts, and garlic chives, in this order, on top of the pork intestines.

Bring the hot pot to a boil over high heat. Decrease the heat to medium and simmer until the vegetables cook down into the broth, about 10 minutes.

Transfer the hot pot to the dining table. Serve the ingredients together with the broth in small bowls.

Suggested shime: *Ramen (page 26).*

PORK KIMCHI HOT POT
Kimuchi Nabe

This dish highlights Korea's contribution to Japanese cuisine, especially in the southern island of Kyushu. Kimchi, of course, is the iconic food of Korea, produced from pickled vegetables and typically spiked with chilies and garlic. We use the most common type of prepared kimchi, made from napa cabbage (called *baechu kimchi* in Korean). Kimchi varies widely by producer, so taste it before you cook, and add more salt or additional dried chilies, if you desire.

SERVES 4

1 cup sake

4 cups water

2 tablespoons shiro miso (page 15)

1 tablespoon soy sauce

1 tablespoon sesame oil

1/2 pound boneless pork shoulder, sliced 1/4 inch thick (ask your butcher, or see "How to Slice Meat for Hot Pot," page 115)

1 pound napa cabbage kimchi, including liquid

1/2 package (about 1/2 pound) firm tofu, cut into 8 pieces

2 ounces daikon, peeled, quartered lengthwise, then cut into 1/4-inch-thick slices

1 clove garlic, finely chopped

2 ounces garlic chives (nira), cut into 3-inch pieces

4 ounces oyster mushrooms, trimmed and pulled apart

3 1/2 ounces (half of a 200-gram package) enoki mushrooms, trimmed and pulled apart

1 negi (page 10), thinly sliced on an angle

Prepare the broth by combining the sake, water, miso, and soy sauce in a bowl, whisking to blend well. Set aside.

Add the sesame oil to a hot pot, and place it over medium heat. When the oil is hot, add the pork, cooking and stirring for 3 minutes. Add the kimchi and its liquid, tofu, daikon, and garlic. Pour in the reserved broth. Increase the heat to high and bring the pot to a boil. Decrease the heat to medium and simmer for 10 minutes. Remove any scum that appears on the surface.

Randomly pile the garlic chives, oyster mushrooms, enoki mushrooms, and *negi* on top of the other ingredients. Simmer for 5 more minutes.

Transfer the hot pot to the dining table. Serve the ingredients together with the broth in small bowls.

Suggested shime: *Mochi (page 27).*

SAKE BREWER HOT POT
Bishu Nabe

The sake breweries of Hiroshima Prefecture, a major sake-producing region, gave birth to this hot pot tradition. Japan's quintessential alcoholic drink, sake is brewed from rice in a process that's closer to making beer than wine. The production season lasts from the fall to the end of winter, during which time back in the old days, workers lived together inside the brewery, away from their families. They're the ones credited with inventing a hot pot that features—what else?—plentiful sake. But it wasn't mere whimsy. While the sake cooks, its alcohol evaporates, leaving an amazing, fragrant essence that permeates the other ingredients. Plus, the pork belly and chicken in the recipe are first seared and caramelized, adding even more delicious notes. Be careful not to ignite the sake's alcohol when you pour it into the hot skillet. Also, use a good, basic *junmai* sake for this dish; you don't need anything fancier. (*Junmai* is a sake quality level and appears on the label.)

SERVES 4

1/4 pound burdock root, cleaned (page 11)

Distilled white vinegar or rice vinegar, for soaking burdock

2 tablespoons sesame oil

4 ounces fresh pork belly, sliced 1/4 inch thick (ask your butcher, or see "How to Slice Meat for Hot Pot," page 115) and halved

2 boneless, skinless chicken breasts (1 1/2 to 2 pounds), cut into 1/4-inch-thick slices

1 (720-ml) bottle sake

1/2 pound napa cabbage, sliced (page 52)

1 negi (page 10), sliced on an angle into 2-inch pieces

1 (7-ounce) package shirataki (page 14), well rinsed, strained, and quartered

4 ounces shiitake mushrooms (about 8 pieces), stems removed

2 teaspoons salt

1/2 cup daikon oroshi (page 18), for garnish

Cut the burdock like you are sharpening the point of a pencil to produce thin shavings. Place the shavings in a bowl of water treated with vinegar (1 cup vinegar per 1 cup of water), so the burdock doesn't oxidize and discolor. Set aside. (Strain before using.)

Place a large skillet (a 12-inch cast-iron skillet is ideal) over medium heat. Add the sesame oil. When the skillet is hot, add the pork belly, cooking and stirring for 1 minute. Add the chicken, cooking and stirring for about 2 minutes, until it turns golden. Add the burdock and cook for 1 minute more, also stirring constantly.

Pour the sake into the skillet, being careful it doesn't ignite and catch fire. Increase the heat to high to bring the skillet to a boil. Decrease the heat to medium and randomly pile in the cabbage, *negi*, *shirataki*, and shiitake mushrooms. Sprinkle the salt over the ingredients. Simmer until the ingredients are cooked through, about 10 minutes.

Transfer the skillet to the dining table. Serve the ingredients together with the broth. Garnish with the *daikon oroshi*.

Suggested shime: Yaki udon *(page 27)*.

LAMB SHABU-SHABU
Lamu Shabu

The northernmost island of Hokkaido is Japan's Big Sky Country, as breathtaking and wide open as Montana. Sheep were introduced there in the nineteenth century, and the region became justly famous for its tender, delectable lamb. In Hokkaido, this meat is usually prepared two ways: as a local grilled dish called "Genghis Khan" (named after the fearsome Mongol emperor, of course) or as shabu-shabu, a nod to the traditional lamb hot pots of Mongolia. The fragrant dipping sauce in the dish bestows a kick lively enough to stand up to lamb's distinctive flavor. Its *tobanjan* is a spicy Chinese fermented bean paste that naturally complements all kinds of meat. Add another tablespoon to the dipping sauce recipe if you like your food flaming hot. Like the other shabu-shabu recipes in the book, cook this one tableside on a portable burner (see "Shabu-Shabu," page 63).

SERVES 4

BLACK SESAME DIPPING SAUCE

1 tablespoon tobanjan

$\frac{1}{4}$ cup mirin

$\frac{1}{4}$ cup soy sauce

2 cloves garlic, grated

2 tablespoons black sesame seed

1 tablespoon sesame oil

$\frac{1}{4}$ cup rice vinegar

1 tablespoon sugar

2 tablespoons coarsely chopped scallions

—

1 pound boneless lamb shoulder or lamb loin, thinly sliced $\frac{1}{8}$ inch thick (ask your butcher, or see "How to Slice Meat for Hot Pot," page 115)

2 ounces garlic chives (nira), cut into 3-inch pieces

$\frac{1}{4}$ small head green cabbage (about $\frac{1}{2}$ pound), cut into bite-size pieces

4 ounces shiitake mushrooms (about 8 pieces), stems removed

4 ounces oyster mushrooms, trimmed and pulled apart

1 negi (page 10), sliced on an angle into 2-inch pieces

2 ounces mung bean sprouts (about 1 cup)

2 (6-inch) pieces kombu

8 cups water, plus more as needed

1 teaspoon salt

To make the dipping sauce, combine the *tobanjan*, mirin, soy sauce, garlic, sesame seed, sesame oil, rice vinegar, sugar, and scallions in the jar of a blender. Pulse until well combined (if you notice a few whole sesame seeds at the end, that's OK). Fill four small bowls with the sauce. Set aside.

Arrange the lamb slices and garlic chives on a serving platter. Arrange the cabbage, shiitake mushrooms, oyster mushrooms, *negi*, and mung bean sprouts on other serving platters.

Set up a portable burner on the dining table, and place a hot pot on top of it. Array the serving platters around the burner. Place bowls with the dipping sauce before each diner.

Place the kombu on the bottom of a hot pot. Add the cabbage, shiitake mushrooms, oyster mushrooms, *negi*, and mung bean sprouts on top of the kombu, arranging each ingredient in a separate, neat bunch. (You can add all of the ingredients at once, or reserve half or more to cook later.) Pour in the 8 cups of water and sprinkle in the salt.

Cover the hot pot and bring it to a boil over high heat. Decrease the heat to medium and simmer for 5 minutes. Uncover the pot and add some of the lamb slices, arranging them in a single layer over the other ingredients. Poach until the lamb slices cook rare or medium rare, 30 seconds to 1 minute. Dip the meat into the black sesame dipping sauce to eat.

Eat in rounds. Poach more lamb in the simmering broth. Add some garlic chives, and cook for 1 minute. Sample the other ingredients, also dipping them into the black sesame sauce. If you reserved some of the tofu and vegetables, add them to the hot pot and cook, as you desire. Add more water to the pot, as needed.

Suggested shime: *Ramen (page 26). Add the black sesame dipping sauce to the broth.*

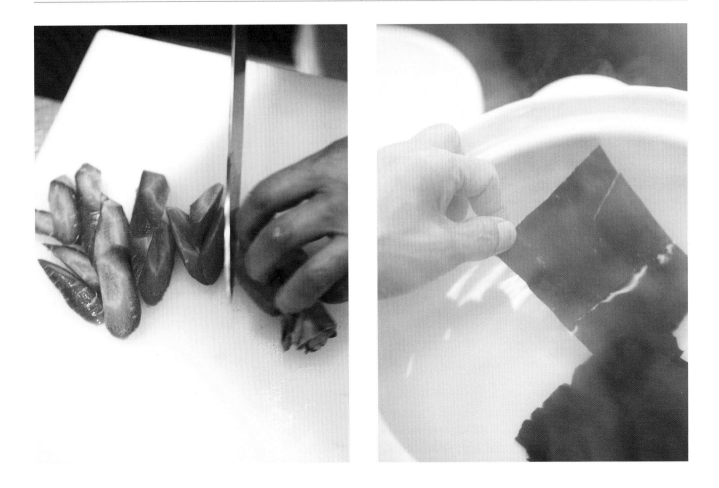

VENISON HOT POT
Momiji Nabe

Although Buddhist edict forbade the eating of four-legged animals in Japan for a millennium, people living deep in the countryside and mountains have hunted game for about just as long. But they adopted euphemisms to make their quarry more socially acceptable. So "mountain whale" became the nom-de-guerre for wild boar, "peony" for boar meat, and "red maple leaf" (*momiji*) the name for venison. Here miso and burdock pair with venison to balance its gaminess, a traditional combination of bold flavors. For the broth, though, we add red wine to give it a contemporary twist, the wine being a natural complement to meat and adding beautiful character. You can also substitute tender beef like rib eye or strip loin for the venison. "Mountain whale" works great with this recipe, too.

SERVES 4

¼ pound burdock root, cleaned (page 11)

Distilled white vinegar or rice vinegar, for soaking burdock

1 (750-ml) bottle red wine like syrah

½ cup Hatcho miso (page 18)

3 small taro roots (about ½ pound), peeled and cut into 1-inch-thick slices

1 tablespoon aka miso (page 18)

½ cup sugar

½ pound napa cabbage, sliced (page 52)

1 (7-ounce) package itokonnyaku (page 14), well rinsed, strained, and quartered

½ package (about 6 ounces) broiled tofu, cut into 4 pieces

4 ounces oyster mushrooms, trimmed and pulled apart

3½ ounces (100-gram package) shimeji mushrooms, trimmed and pulled apart

1 negi (page 10), sliced on an angle into 2-inch pieces

1 pound venison loin or other tender part, cut into ¼-inch-thick slices (ask your butcher, or see "How to Slice Meat for Hot Pot," page 115)

2 cups shungiku leaves (page 11), stemmed

Coarsely ground black pepper, for accent

Slice the burdock into 1-inch pieces by cutting on an angle and rolling the root a quarter turn after each slice. Place the pieces in a bowl of water treated with vinegar (1 teaspoon vinegar per 1 cup of water), so the burdock doesn't oxidize and discolor. (Strain before using.)

Place the burdock on the bottom of a hot pot and pour in the red wine. Cover the pot and bring it to a boil over high heat. Uncover the pot, decrease the heat to medium, and simmer for 15 minutes.

While the hot pot is simmering, use a knife to cut the dense *Hatcho* miso into small pieces, about the size of ¼-inch cubes.

After the pot has simmered for 15 minutes, randomly pile the taro root into the hot pot. Spoon the *Hatcho* miso, *aka* miso, and sugar into the broth, in the center of the pot. Cover and simmer for 5 minutes. (The miso and sugar will dissolve into the broth while they cook.) Uncover the pot, push the burdock and taro root to one side, and add the cabbage, *itokonnyaku*, and tofu, arranging each ingredient in a separate, neat bunch. Cover and simmer for 5 minutes more.

Uncover the pot and add the oyster mushrooms, *shimeji* mushrooms, *negi*, and venison to the hot pot, arranging in neatly ordered bunches beside the other ingredients. Simmer for 5 to 10 minutes, depending if you like the venison cooked rare or medium. Use chopsticks to press the venison into the broth as it cooks. Add the *shungiku* leaves to one side of the hot pot and simmer for 1 minute more.

Transfer the hot pot to the dining table. Serve the ingredients together with the broth in small bowls, accenting with the black pepper.

Suggested shime: Yaki udon *(page 27).*

TABLESIDE COOKING OPTION: Arrange the ingredients on serving platters. After the burdock simmers in the red wine for 15 minutes, do all the cooking at the dining table. Add the supporting ingredients all at once, or reserve half or more to cook later. Cook a little of the venison at a time.

"POTLUCK" HOT POT

We have our potluck dinners, Japanese have their *yami nabe*—same thing, except in a hot pot. This is one you have to cook tableside on a portable burner. You set up a hot pot with foundation ingredients and a soy sauce broth (use the one in "Anything Goes" Hot Pot, page 89). Your guests bring whatever ingredients they want to prepare, add them to the hot pot, and go to town. There's also another version of this dish, but with a little wrinkle: You eat it in the dark—so you can't see what your friends are sticking in. It can get a little bizarre, yes, but a lot of fun, and is—no surprise—especially popular in Japanese college dorms. Just make sure to set some ground rules first.

Resources

JAPANESE INGREDIENTS

You can find Japanese ingredients and produce at Asian markets from coast to coast. The following is a list of Japanese supermarkets and markets online and across the country, plus Asian supermarket chains that carry a wide selection of Japanese foods.

Online

Asian Food Grocer
www.asianfoodgrocer.com

Mitsuwa
www.mitsuwa.com/english

National and Regional Chains

H-Mart
A Korean supermarket chain with stores nationwide. Check their website for the location nearest you.
www.hmart.com

99 Ranch Market
A Chinese supermarket chain with 28 stores in four states. Check their website for the location nearest you.
www.99ranch.com

California

Ebisu Supermarket
Fountain Valley
www.ocebisu.com

Marukai
Supermarket chain with eight locations in Northern and Southern California
www.marukai.com

Mitsuwa
Supermarket with six locations in Northern and Southern California
www.mitsuwa.com/english

Nijiya Market
Market with ten locations in Northern and Southern California
www.nijiya.com

Super Mira Market
San Francisco
(415) 921-6529

Tokyo Fish Market
Albany
(510) 524-7243

Colorado

Pacific Mercantile Company
Denver
www.pacificeastwest.com

Illinois

Mitsuwa
Arlington Heights
www.mitsuwa.com/english

Sea Ranch Grocery
Wilmette
(847) 256-7010

Tensuke Market
Elk Grove Village
www.tensuke.us

Maryland

Daruma Japanese Market
Bethesda
www.darumajapanmarket.com

Massachusetts

Kotobukiya
Cambridge
www.kotobukiyamarket.com

Michigan

Koyama Shoten
Livonia
(734) 464-1480

One World Market
Novi
(248) 374-0844

New Jersey

Daido Market
Fort Lee
www.daidomarket.com

Mitsuwa
Edgewater
www.mitsuwa.com/english

New York

Daido Market
White Plains
www.daidomarket.com

Fuji Mart
Scarsdale
(914) 472-1510

JAS Mart
New York
(212) 866-4780

Katagiri
New York
www.katagiri.com

Nijiya Market
Hartsdale
www.nijiya.com

Sunrise Mart
Two locations in New York
(212) 598-3040

Ohio

Tensuke Market
Columbus
www.tensukemarket.com

Oregon
Uwajimaya
Beaverton
www.uwajimaya.com

Pennsylvania
Maido
Narbeth
www.maidookini.com

Tokyo Japanese Store
Pittsburgh
www.tokyostorepgh.com

Texas
Daido Market
Houston
www.daidomarket.com

Shop Minoya
Plano
(972) 769-8346

Virginia
Naniwa Foods
McLean
(703) 893-7209

Washington
Uwajimaya
Markets in Seattle and Bellevue
www.uwajimaya.com

SEAFOOD, POULTRY, AND MEAT
These provisioners offer top-quality ingredients online.

Flying Pigs Farm
Heritage pork
www.flyingpigsfarm.com

Heritage Foods USA
Heritage chicken, duck, pork, beef, and lamb raised on small farms
www.heritagefoodsusa.com

The Lobster Place
Wide variety of seafood
www.lobsterplace.com

Niman Ranch
All-natural chicken, pork, beef, and lamb
www.nimanranch.com

Pike Place Fish Market
Wide variety of seafood
www.pikeplacefish.com

Vital Choice Wild Seafood
Wild salmon, halibut, black cod, and scallops
www.vitalchoice.com

Index